D251 BLOCK 2 UNITS 5 AND 6
SOCIAL SCIENCES: A SECOND LEVEL COURSE
D251 ISSUES IN DEAFNESS

DEAF PEOPLE
IN HEARING WORLDS

INTRODUCTION TO BLOCK 2

UNIT 5
EDUCATION AND DEAF PEOPLE: LEARNING TO COMMUNICATE OR COMMUNICATING TO LEARN?

PREPARED FOR THE COURSE TEAM BY SUSAN GREGORY, JANICE SILO AND LARAINE CALLOW

UNIT 6
THE MANUFACTURE OF DISADVANTAGE

PREPARED FOR THE COURSE TEAM BY GEORGE TAYLOR AND CARLO LAURENZI

PAINTING ON COVER AND TITLE PAGE BY TREVOR LANDELL

D1464272

The Open University

THIS COURSE HAS BEEN PRODUCED WITH FUNDING FROM THE DEPARTMENT OF HEALTH

D251 Core Course Team

ANNE DARBY Diploma Placements Officer, Faculty of Social Sciences

SUSAN GREGORY Senior Lecturer in Psychology, Faculty of Social Sciences (Course Team Chair)

YVONNE HOLMES Secretary, Faculty of Social Sciences

LINDA JANES Course Manager, Faculty of Social Sciences

GEORGE TAYLOR Lecturer in Interdisciplinary Social Sciences, Faculty of Social Sciences

Other Open University Contributors

JULIET BISHOP Research Fellow in Social Sciences, Faculty of Social Sciences

DEBBIE CROUCH Designer

TIM DANT Research Fellow in Health and Social Welfare, Continuing Education

VIC FINKELSTEIN Senior Lecturer in Health and Social Welfare, Continuing Education

GERALD HALES Research Fellow, Institute of Educational Technology

FIONA HARRIS Editor

KEITH HOWARD Graphic Artist

MARY JOHN Senior Lecturer in Psychology, Faculty of Social Sciences

VIC LOCKWOOD BBC Producer

KEN PATTON BBC Producer

ALISON TUCKER BBC Producer

External Consultants

LORNA ALLSOP Centre for Deaf Studies, University of Bristol

LARAINE CALLOW Consultant in Deafness

MARY FIELDER National Council of Social Workers with Deaf People

GILLIAN M. HARTLEY Teacher, Thorn Park School, Bradford

LYNNE HAWCROFT Royal National Institute for the Deaf

JIM KYLE Centre for Deaf Studies, University of Bristol

PADDY LADD London Deaf Video Project

CARLO LAURENZI National Deaf Children's Society

CLIVE MASON Presenter, BBC 'See Hear'

RUKHSANA MEHERALI Educational Psychologist, Royal School for the Deaf, Derby

DOROTHY MILES Writer, Lecturer and Poet

BOB PECKFORD British Deaf Association

CHRISTINE PLAYER Tutor Adviser

SHARON RIDGEWAY National Council of Social Workers with Deaf People

JANICE SILO Teacher of the Deaf, Derbyshire

External Assessors

MARY BRENNAN Co-director, MA and Advanced Diploma in Sign Language Studies, University of Durham

MALCOLM PAYNE Head of Department of Applied Community Studies, Manchester Polytechnic

Sign Language Interpreters

BYRON CAMPBELL

ELIZABETH JONES

KYRA POLLITT

LINDA RICHARDS

The Open University
Walton Hall, Milton Keynes
MK7 6AB

First published 1991 Reprinted 1992, 1995

Copyright © 1991 The Open University

Designed by the Graphic Design Group of the Open University

Printed in the United Kingdom by The Open University

ISBN 0 7492 0051 0

This publication forms part of the Open University course D251 Issues in Deafness. If you have not enrolled on the course and would like to buy this or other Open University material, please write to Open University Educational Enterprises Ltd, 12 Cofferidge Close, Stony Stratford, Milton Keynes MK11 1BY, United Kingdom. If you wish to enquire about enrolling as an Open University student, please write to the Admissions Office, The Open University, P.O. Box 48, Walton Hall, Milton Keynes MK7 6AB, United Kingdom.

Introduction to Block 2

In Block 2 we change our perspective. Rather than looking at Deaf people, their community, language and culture in their own right, we now move on to look at deaf people in the context of the hearing world. We do this through the examination of deaf people within three of the major systems that have had an impact upon their lives: education, psychological assessment and social welfare.

Unit 5 on education represents a significant shift in emphasis from that of Block 1. Within the educational processes, the responsibility of those who provide services for deaf children, extends to all children with a hearing loss. Thus children who will grow up to become members of the Deaf community are considered alongside children with minor hearing losses. As will be seen in the unit, this is an important factor in the forms of provision that are made.

In Unit 6 the impact of the hearing world is discussed by a consideration of the way in which deaf people are presented stereotypically, in a manner similar to other members of minority groups. Such stereotypes have implications for the ways in which deaf people are treated by society, and the unit examines the impact of these views on deaf people as patients of mental health services.

The greatest impact of professional groups on adult Deaf people is probably within the social services. For, until recently, specialist social workers were one of the only professions trained to work with Deaf people, and their power and influence went beyond that which would traditionally be thought of as part of the social services domain. How this came about and how this has affected the lives of Deaf people are themes for Unit 7.

While the three systems described in the three units are located within different institutions within the hearing world, they share certain features with respect to Deaf people. They all represent ways of viewing deafness from an essentially hearing perspective, where the issue of 'not hearing' rather than 'being Deaf' dominates the understanding. Deafness is seen as a problem and hearing people have the power and make the decisions. As you work through these units you should actively contrast them with the view of deafness put forward in Block 1.

Unit 5 Education and Deaf People: Learning to Communicate or Communicating to Learn?

prepared for the course team by Susan Gregory, Janice Silo and Laraine Callow

Contents

Associated study materials

Video Two, *Sign Language*.

Reader One, Article 1, 'Janet's Diary', Janet Goodwill.

Reader One, Section 3, *The Pre-School Years*.

Reader One, Section 4, *School-Days*.

Reader One, Article 12, 'A Polytechnic with a Difference', Lucy Briggs.

Reader One, Article 13, 'Education for Life?', Christopher Reid.

Reader One, Article 14, 'Training to Teach', Sarah Elsey.

Reader One, Article 15, 'A Career in Design', Richard Shaw.

Reader One, Article 16, 'From College to Work in the Lace Industry', Paul Holehouse.

Reader One, Article 19, 'A Deaf Teacher: A Personal Odyssey', Janice Silo.

Reader Two, Section 5, *Educational Perspectives: Learning to Communicate or Communicating to Learn?*

Reader Two, Article 7.7, 'Deaf People and Minority Groups in the UK', Jim Kyle.

Set Book: J. Kyle, and B. Woll, *Sign Language: The Study of Deaf People and Their Language*, Chapters 11 and 12.

D251 Issues in Deafness

Readers
Reader One: Taylor, G. and Bishop, J. (eds) (1990) *Being Deaf: The Experience of Deafness*, London, Pinter Publishers.
Reader Two: Gregory, S. and Hartley, G.M. (eds) (1990) *Constructing Deafness*, London, Pinter Publishers.

Set Books
Kyle, J. and Woll, B. (1985) *Sign Language: The Study of Deaf People and Their Language*, Cambridge, Cambridge University Press.
Miles, D. (1988) *British Sign Language: A Beginner's Guide*, London, BBC Books (BBC Enterprises). With a chapter by Paddy Ladd.

Videotapes
Video One   *Sandra's Story: The History of a Deaf Family*
Video Two   *Sign Language*
Video Three   *Deaf People and Mental Health*
Video Four   *Signs of Change: Politics and the Deaf Community*

Objectives

After studying this unit you should be able to:

1 Describe the impact of the educational system for deaf children on the Deaf community and suggest changes that the Deaf community might wish to see in the system.

2 Suggest why Deaf people have had such a limited role in the education of deaf children and discuss how changes could be brought about, and the consequences of such changes.

3 Give an account of the debate concerning methods of communication and the education of deaf children and the effect of this debate within education.

4 Give reasons for and against the education of deaf children in mainstream education.

5 Describe the attainments of deaf children within the current educational system and suggest reasons why these are so low.

6 Understand the dilemmas faced by hearing parents of deaf children in making decisions about their children's education.

7 Appreciate the special issues that surround the education of deaf children from ethnic minority groups.

Study guide

Week one
Study the Introduction and Sections 1–3. You will find it useful to orientate yourself to this unit by spending time reflecting upon deaf people's accounts of their own education in Reader One and on Video Two, Sequences 4 and 5. You should then go on to look at the debates concerning language and communication in the education of deaf children. Do not be too concerned if you do not complete all the reading from Reader Two at this stage—you will have time to review this again in week 3.

Week two
Study Sections 4–5. These sections ask you to look at how education for deaf children is organized and at the impact of policies of integration.

Week three
Study Sections 6–8. Here you will look at various perspectives on education: those of Deaf people, parents and consumers. You will find it useful to review Section 3 on language and communication in the light of these various perspectives.

Introduction

My experience of mainstreaming in England, however, leads me to believe that it is the most dangerous move yet against the early development of a deaf person's character, self-confidence and basic sense of identity.

(Ladd, 1981, in Reader One)

I remember that when I had biology classes I used to ask questions about various things. The teacher could never understand what I was asking so my friend had to interpret for me by means of voicing my questions again ... They really tried to help. If they had used Sign Language they would have known what I was asking, and saved me some embarrassment. Looking back I have to wonder—who had the problem?

(Craddock, 1990, in Reader One)

From your reading of the course so far, you will have realized that the education of deaf children is a controversial topic—and one on which feelings run high. It is a theme which pervades almost all discussion of issues in deafness, and you will have already encountered a number of perspectives on the debates from the units, videos and Reader articles you have studied to date. Unit 1 introduced you to deaf people's accounts of their own lives, including several different perspectives on education. In Video One, which you watched in conjunction with Unit 1, Sandra pointed out how important she felt boarding school to be in her children's education, and in giving them a sense of identity. This is reiterated in Unit 2, where the negative effects, on the Deaf community, of mainstreaming or integration in education are discussed. In Unit 3, which focuses on language, the issue for parents as to whether to use sign or spoken language with their children was considered. Video Two, which was viewed with Unit 3, included the LASER conference on bilingualism in education as a focus for the discussion on interpreting. We shall return to a discussion on bilingual approaches in Section 3.3, when we look at communication and education. Unit 4 concluded with a description of the plight of deaf young people, who have received an oral education in which sign language has not been used, and have left school with competence neither in spoken language nor in sign language, and find it difficult to identify with either the Deaf or hearing worlds.

You may have come to the course with strong ideas on the education of deaf children, and you may have developed your opinions through your study of the course so far. Those views are likely to be informed by your relationship to the Deaf community, whether you are deaf yourself, a parent of a deaf child or a professional working with deaf people. In this unit we wish to present a range of views on the education of deaf children, and examine what lies behind those views. We will also look at these issues within the wider social and educational context.

You will find in this unit that 'deaf' (with a small 'd') is often used rather than 'Deaf' (with a capital 'D'), and in fact the Deaf/deaf distinction has become more problematic. As we move from looking at Deaf people and their community to deaf people in a hearing world, we inevitably find ourselves in an area where deafness is more likely to be defined audiologically. This is even the more so in a unit which focuses on education, and thus on deaf children.

The reason that a deaf child comes under the remit of the specialist educational services is made on audiological criteria, not on cultural or attitudinal ones. For this reason we shall use 'deaf' to refer to these children throughout. While it may be thought that schools for the deaf are centres of the Deaf community, to use 'Deaf' for pupils attending these would mean that every change of school could involve a deaf/Deaf switch, and could become nonsensical. 'Deaf' with a capital 'D' is only used in this unit when the group being described has a clear identification with the Deaf community.

1 The views of deaf people

In this section we would like you to re-read, read for the first time, and view some accounts by deaf people of their own education. In doing this we would like you to address the following questions:

1   What do deaf people see as the main educational issues?

2   How does each one identify him- or herself with these main issues?

3   From your own perspective, what comment would you offer on the views put forward?

◀ Reading
Read or re-read the following articles from Reader One:

Article 1, 'Janet's Diary' by Janet Goodwill;

Article 8, 'School—the Early Years' by Christine Monery and Linda Janes;

Article 9, 'School Experiences' by Clive Mason;

Article 10, 'Making Plans for Nigel: The Erosion of Identity by Mainstreaming' by Paddy Ladd;

Article 11, 'Life at Secondary School' by Elizabeth Craddock;

Article 12, 'A Polytechnic with a Difference', by Lucy Briggs;

Article 13, 'Education for Life?' by Christopher Reid;

Article 14, 'Training to Teach' by Sarah Elsey;

Article 15, 'A Career in Design' by Richard Shaw;

Article 16, 'From College to Work in the Lace Industry' by Paul Holehouse. ◀

◀ Video
You should watch Video Two, Sequences 4 and 5, and in particular the accounts by Sandra and Wendy of their own school days. ◀

A number of issues emerge from these readings and from the video sequences, but they can probably be subsumed under three main headings:

1 Should deaf children be educated alongside hearing children, or in special schools?
2 Should sign language be used in the education of deaf children?
3 Can deaf children receive an appropriate education from hearing teachers?

The answers to these questions may seem linked, but this is not inevitably so, as the discussion in this unit will reveal.

A whole range of views has emerged on these three points. The accounts you have just read and viewed come from a variety of perspectives, from those who went to mainstream schools on the one hand, to those who went to special schools on the other. All those who went to special schools put forward a positive case for their role in establishing Deaf identity. The problems of being left at school at an early age and missing their family (Christine Monery, Janet Goodwill) and losing contact with neighbourhood friends (Lucy Briggs) are described. However, the overall picture is a positive one, with some even saying they preferred being at school to being at home (Clive Mason, Lucy Briggs). Of those who attended mainstream schools, Paddy Ladd paints a vivid picture of the 'erosion of his identity', step-by-step, because his deafness made him unable to participate in school life. On the other hand, Richard Shaw and Sarah Elsey, who were educated in mainstream settings, do not feel they would have been happier at a school for the deaf; though, while they describe their school days positively, Sarah does report isolation and being teased. Lucy Briggs is interesting in that she, of her own choice, moved from a special school to a mainstream school for her A-levels, because she felt this would 'improve my communication skills and increase my confidence'. While she reports that this did indeed happen, she also felt that friendships there were 'superficial compared to my relationships at St John's [Special School]'.

All the pupils were educated orally, as was the practice throughout the country until recently, although those at special school developed sign language outside the classroom and for many this was where real education took place (Wendy Daunt, Sandra, Christine Monery, Clive Mason). Some describe the negative attitudes towards sign language inculcated in the education system, which they feel they have had to overcome (Christopher Reid). However, for others sign language did not appear to be an issue, and the oral approach was accepted (Sarah Elsey, Richard Shaw). It may be argued that for these two their hearing loss put them in a different category and they were able to make good use of hearing aids and other equipment. The fact that children with a range of hearing losses come under the auspices of services for deaf children will be an issue we will discuss later in the unit.

Apart from the details of their education, what also emerges from these accounts is the depth of feeling and concern that Deaf people have about education. Yet this group has never been given a voice in educational policy and decision making. Whatever we feel about any of the issues (and they are complex), it still remains an indictment that the decisions have been made in the hearing context and by hearing people. There are many hearing people who feel they have the best interests of deaf children at heart—but is this enough?

In examining the various debates on the education of deaf children, we shall be entering a domain in which hearing people have had a major influence on the lives of deaf people, and the absence, or denial, of the Deaf perspective in these debates must be regarded as one of the more significant features. At the end of the unit we will return to the views of deaf people by looking at a study of young deaf people and their own accounts of their education.

2 The failure of deaf education

Before going on to consider the debates and discussions in the education of deaf children, we should examine one of the main factors in the debate, the perceived failure of the education of deaf children in conventional academic terms.

In the mid-1970s Conrad and his associates embarked on a study to look at the attainments of deaf school-leavers (Conrad, 1979a). (This study is reported in Reader Two, Article 5.4.) To do this they tested all children receiving special educational provision because of hearing loss, who were of school-leaving age (in practice, those between 15 and $16\frac{1}{2}$ years) at the time of testing. Some were excluded because they had other disabilities or their deafness was of late onset, leaving a sample of 468. The study investigated a number of areas including reading ability, lip-reading and speech intelligibility. All the school-leavers were examined on a standard test of reading ability and the results were reported in terms of median scores. The median score is the score in which half the children score higher, and half score lower. Thus the median reading age of the whole sample was 9.0 years, meaning that half of the sample could read better than an average 9-year-old, and half could not read as well. As an approximate guide, a minimum reading age of 11 years is generally held to be necessary to read tabloid newspapers.

If we consider first those children whose reading age was the same or better than their chronological (actual) age, for the least deaf children this was only 8 per cent, but for the deaf group it dropped to 2.4 per cent (5 out of 205). We shall refer again to these five teenagers in Section 3.6.1. If we look at those children who had virtually no reading comprehension at all and were functionally illiterate, we find this included 25 per cent of the less deaf group and 50 per cent of the deaf group. Thus for those children with substantial losses, half were leaving school unable to read.

In Unit 1 some of the inherent difficulties in lip-reading were described. Yet because much of the explicit teaching of deaf children was designed to develop their lip-reading skills, Conrad also examined the lip-reading ability of the deaf students. A comparison group of seventy-five hearing children was taken and white noise was passed through headphones to make them effectively deaf. In fact, they would have been deafer than the deaf students. An adaptation of the Donaldson test was used in which the speaker makes a statement, and the subject has to indicate to which of six to nine pictures the statement refers. The ability to understand speech through lip-reading was exactly the same for the two groups. The 10 years of training and practice in lip-reading of the deaf students led to no objectively verifiable effect. Alternatively, it may be that a good understanding of spoken English is as important for lip-reading as specific training.

The third main area assessed by Conrad was that of speech intelligibility. Head teachers were asked to give their evaluation of this, based on their knowledge of the school-leaver, rather than on a particular sample of speech. They were asked to attempt to do it from the point of view of inexperienced listeners. Clearly, teachers of deaf children are much more likely to find the speech of their own pupils intelligible and thus, despite the instructions, any bias will be in favour of greater intelligibility.

Taking the children in schools for the deaf, the following ratings were obtained:

Wholly intelligible	14%
Fairly easy to understand	20%
About half understood	18%
Very hard to understand	25%
Effectively unintelligible	23%

Thus there would be little difficulty in holding a spoken conversation with about one-third of the children, but it would be extremely difficult to do so with almost half of them. It is not surprising that the least deaf children had the more intelligible speech.

While the results of the study were not surprising to educators working with young deaf children at that time, the documenting of the attainments of such a large group had a major impact, and it is one of the most often quoted references on the education of deaf children. The study took place some years ago and there are those who would maintain that things have changed with better technical support and so forth. However, no later studies have demonstrated adequately that there is an improvement. More recent work on reading (Wood et al., 1986a) and speech intelligibility (Markides, 1983a) show much the same results. Also, such results are not unique to the UK and are confirmed by research throughout the Western World, including the USA, Holland, Denmark and Sweden.

A recent major study from the USA begins with the words:

> The education of deaf students in the United States is not as it should be. It has been documented time upon time that deaf children lag substantially behind their hearing age mates in virtually all measures of academic achievement.
>
> (Johnson et al., 1989)

◀ Activity 1
You may or may not have been surprised by these results. We would like you to note your reaction, and also reflect on the following questions:

Δ   What are the goals of the education of deaf children as established by this study?
Δ   What should be the goals of the education of deaf children?

If you are deaf, consider this from your own point of view and also that of hearing people—perhaps the hearing parent of a deaf child. If you are hearing, consider the views that deaf people might have, and their feelings about Conrad's work. ◀

◀ Comment
It is clear that it is implicit in the measures taken by Conrad that the purpose of the education of deaf children is to prepare them for a hearing world. (We are not ascribing this view to Conrad himself; he has used measures that were generally acceptable to argue a particular case about the failure of deaf education.) ◀

The questions to be posed by this unit are:

Δ   Why are the attainments of deaf children so low?
Δ   How has a system of education, which has been the subject of so much discussion and research, and which has been significantly researched, come to fail so dramatically?

How you answered the question 'What should be the goals of the education of deaf children?' in Activity 1 will colour your reading of this unit.

3 Language and communication in the education of deaf children

3.1 Oralism

The work of Conrad, and the accounts of their education by deaf young people, all took place under the aegis of the oralist philosophy which maintains that spoken language should be the medium of education and that sign language should be prohibited.

◀ Reading
From Reader Two, you should now read:

Article 5.5, 'A Critical Examination of Different Approaches to Communication in the Education of Deaf Children' by Wendy Lynas, Alan Huntington and Ivan Tucker.

This is a modern statement of the oralist position. ◀

◀ Activity 2
You should list arguments advocated for the oralist position and note your response to them. ◀

From what you have studied so far, many of you will be surprised at the oralist view. Given what you know about Deaf people, their language and culture, it seems absurd that sign language should not be used in the educational context. To some Deaf people oralism is an obscenity, and there have been discussions as to how oralism should be included in the course. It could be that its very inclusion legitimates it in some way.

However, in considering what happens in the education of deaf people it is important to understand:

Δ   how oralism came about

Δ   why oralism is still so pervasive.

3.1.1 The 1880 Milan Conference

The critical event in the history of oralism must be the Milan Conference of 1880. This is usually seen as the beginning of the formal assertive oralist movement in Europe, although there are indications of a shift towards oralism before this time.

The events surrounding the Milan Conference can be described in a number of different ways. There are many histories that can be written of deaf education and, while we try to explore these, they can only be partial views.

The first international congress on the education of deaf children was a small affair with only twenty-seven participants and held in Paris in 1878. The second congress, the Milan Conference, attracted 164 participants. The following motions were passed at that conference:

> 1 The Congress, considering the incontestable superiority of speech over signs for restoring deaf mutes to social life and for giving them greater facility in language, declares that the method of articulation should have preference over that of signs in the instruction and education of the deaf and dumb.

> 2 Considering that the simultaneous use of signs and speech has the disadvantage of injuring speech, lip-reading and the precision of ideas, the Congress declares that the pure oral method ought to be preferred.

◀ Reading
You should now read the account of the congress in Article 5.3, 'Why the Deaf Are Angry' by Harlan Lane in Reader Two. ◀

Lane emphasizes the way in which major decisions were made by a relatively small number of people (164), seven-eighths of whom were French or Italian and committed to oral methods. The British delegate was Thomas Arnold and all the delegates except one were hearing.

The ripples from this conference went out in all directions. One direct consequence, which had a major impact, was the removal of most deaf teachers from the education of deaf children. Not only did this have implications for deaf children in terms of the models available to them, but it also removed deaf people from positions of power regarding decisions about deaf children.

A particularly poignant speech, reported by Lane in his book *When the Mind Hears*, was given at the time when the National Institution for the Deaf in Paris had to sack the deaf teachers 'whose only fault is to be deaf'. The contribution of these teachers is recalled, with affection:

> ... you, ... who despite the absence of sense rendered so much service not only to your class but to the general progress of our teaching. None, among your hearing colleagues contributed more to the preparation of our curriculum.
>
> (Lane, 1988)

and of another:

> ... you have repaid one hundred fold your debt to this institution by giving in turn to the young generations who came after you the knowledge you acquired here.
>
> (Ibid.)

In the UK, school records give evidence suggesting that deaf teachers were sacked, and that teachers were employed, for whom not knowing signs was an advantage. The Minute Books of the Margate branch of the London Asylum (now the Royal School for the Deaf, Margate) of 1880 note that the following advertisement was to be inserted in the *Schoolmaster* and the *National Society Paper*:

> Wanted, two male and two female teachers for deaf and dumb Asylum. Required to teach orally, must not have been previously engaged in teaching signing. No deaf experience necessary.

Later, on the same page of the Minute Book, it was resolved to dispense with three teachers:

Phillips	3 months notice	1 year salary
Smith	3 months notice	6 months salary
Clarke	1 months notice	—

The large amount of compensation for the first two teachers would seem to imply that they had been at the school a long time. Why were they sacked? Was it to make room for oral teachers?

Yet, the Milan Conference was not the sudden dramatic event that it might appear to have been. In fact, moves to oralist methods were already well in hand prior to 1880, as will be discussed below. Moreover, although the consequences for the Deaf community may have been oppressive, the intention, certainly of some of the decision makers, was to bring education to deaf children, rather than leaving them isolated in the large institutions which were home for so many deaf children at that time.

Figure 5.1 Illustration of Asylum at The Old Kent Road, London. This school was later moved to Margate and became The Royal School for the Deaf
(Source: courtesy of the Royal National Institute for the Deaf)

The 1880 Milan Conference must be seen in its context. It was held at a time when there was a move in Europe towards education for all. In the UK, the passing of the Elementary Education Act of 1870 established the principle of universal education which, as the Chairman of the School Board, Sir Charles Reed, pointed out, should include deaf children. The *formal* inclusion of deaf children came with the Education Act of 1893 which extended the provisions of the 1870 Act to 'deaf, dumb and blind children' with adaptations to meet their special circumstances. Before this, education for deaf children had been purely voluntary and dependent upon charitable institutions. In the first half of the nineteenth century, there were large institutions for 'deaf and dumb' children in Edinburgh, Aberdeen, Glasgow, Birmingham, Manchester, Liverpool, Doncaster, Brighton, Exeter and Bristol which were opened mainly at the instigation of philanthropists. The main goal was to provide shelter from the world and to give spiritual education and care. An overriding concern was to keep the children alive and free from illness, as is apparent from reading through the record books of the schools. Increasingly, however, the large institutions were criticized, not only in the UK but also in France and Italy: with the advent of universal education, the promise of oralism was seen as a way of bringing these children into the education system, and of rescuing them from these large asylums.

Oralism was already established in Europe and had a long history there. As was mentioned in Unit 1, the first teacher of the deaf is generally held to be Pablo Ponce de Leon (1520–1584), a Benedictine monk who established a school to tutor deaf children of the Spanish nobility. At that time it was necessary to read and write in order to inherit land. It is reputed that de Leon's first student was Don Francisco Velasco, the eldest son of the House of Tudor, who would have been denied his inheritance had he not learnt to read and write. De Leon appears to have had great success but little is known of his methods. As Moores points out, the communication style attributed to him seems to depend on the writer's own preference:

> There is a tendency for those who favour the use of signs to believe that he did (Arnold 1879, Hodgson 1954) and for those who oppose signs to believe that he did not (Bender 1970).
>
> (Moores, 1978)

After the death of de Leon there is a gap, with teaching of the deaf re-emerging in Spain 30 years later with Juan Bonet and Ramirez de Carrion. In 1620 Bonet published the first book written on teaching the deaf, *The Education of Letters and the Art of Teaching the Mute to Speak*. Bonet was an inspired teacher, although has been criticized for not acknowledging the influence of de Carrion and de Leon in his writings. He advocated the use of the one-handed manual alphabet, and advocated that all members of the family of the deaf person learn manual communication. He also stressed the importance of early intervention. The influence of these Spanish pioneers spread throughout Europe and there are accounts of individual teachers working with deaf children throughout the seventeenth century.

In Germany, Samuel Heinecke established the school in Leipzig in 1778. He did not believe in the use of signs and felt that thought arose from speech. This emphasis on speech and speech training was to become known as the 'German method'. Gradually, German teachers came to the UK, as well as going to Holland and Italy, and from 1860 there were a number of isolated initiatives to bring these methods to the UK. In 1862 a private school for deaf children was opened in London using the oral methods of the German system. In 1866 the Jewish School adopted oral methods, and by the middle of the 1870s several schools for the deaf had opened. In 1877 a conference of headmasters of institutions for the deaf was held in London, at which the main topic was the need for reforming institutions. This led to one resignation: that of James Watson, head of the Asylum in the Old Kent Road. Thus by 1880, schools in the UK were already looking to oral methods. The National Association of Teachers of the Deaf (NATD) was formed in 1885, as was the College of Teachers. Both were concerned to raise the status of deaf education with an emphasis on oral methods. Even at that time the debate about communication methods was fierce.

◀ Reading
You should now read Article 5.2, 'The Teaching of Speech: Historical Developments' by Andreas Markides in Reader Two, which gives an oralist perspective on the Milan Conference. You should contrast this with the account by Lane which you read earlier.[1] ◀

[1] The early history of the education of deaf children is fascinating, and accounts can be found in Lane (1988) and McLoughlin (1987) for those students wishing to read further. These texts are not, however, a requirement for the course.

3.1.2 Oralism today

The events surrounding the Milan Conference are clearly complex, but what is more important is to examine the reasons why the philosophy of oralism persists today.

◀ Activity 3
Make notes for yourself on some of the possible reasons for this. ◀

◀ Comment
(a) The organization of provision

Services for deaf children, or for hearing-impaired children as they are usually known, are responsible for all children with a hearing loss. Some of these children have minor hearing losses and oral approaches are appropriate, particularly in conjunction with good hearing aids. However, policies with respect to these children have been seen as appropriate across the whole range of hearing loss, including children who seem to have quite different requirements. While it would seem that the variation within the group of all children with a hearing loss is so great as to imply the need for differing approaches to education, oralists argue that oralism can and should be extended to all.

This, of course, raises further issues. Why are services arranged in this way? Who makes these decisions? What impact has the Deaf community on education decisions? You will find these issues discussed, from a Deaf perspective, in Unit 9.

(b) The promise of technology

During the twentieth century there have been massive technological advances in hearing aids. This has enabled children with certain degrees of hearing loss to make effective use of their hearing when previously they could not do so. It has been argued that initially all children have some residual hearing which can be utilized; however, many Deaf people dispute this. This is discussed further in Section 4.3.

(c) 'Scientific' approaches to language development

The past decades have seen an explosion in the study of language and language development. Theories of language acquisition have been appropriated into the education of deaf children. Because the approaches to language in the education of deaf children thus seemed to be validated by psychological experiments, they acquired status, although the original research was all done with hearing children. At an earlier stage the idea was to break language down into elements, team these and then blend them together. Later studies focused on the language that hearing children received. These approaches were then applied to deaf children. Thus lately the concern has been that deaf children do not hear enough spoken language, that if the input was adequate then language would develop—the message has been TALK, TALK, TALK. By utilizing studies of language development in hearing children, which has focused on aspects of spoken language, an oral approach has seemed possible and validated by scientific studies.

Figure 5.2   Using a speech trainer
(Source: courtesy of the Royal National Institute for the Deaf)

(d) The status of sign language

Unit 3 described how it has only been since the late 1960s that sign languages have been appreciated as true languages. The possibility of sign language being the medium of education is therefore a relatively new idea. Before this, sign languages were perceived as crude systems of mime and gesture; they seemed irrelevant to the education process.

(e) The normalization principle

Within the auspices of the education system, deaf children are considered as disabled, and normalization is the goal. The whole notion of normalization, the need to approximate to the 'normal' as far as possible, is discussed in detail in Section 5. Oralists argue that only oralism gives deaf people access to the hearing world and that any use of signing could inhibit this. In fact, many advocates of the use of signing in education see it as a route to the hearing world.

(f) The training of teachers

Because of the strong hold that oralism has had on the education of deaf children, until recently sign language was not part of the curriculum for those training to be teachers of the deaf, and in some institutions it was actively discouraged. Deaf people, as well as being under-represented in the profession, have not been included among the trainers. Training has largely been undertaken by hearing people with little or no contact with, or understanding of, the Deaf community, its language or culture.

(g) The wishes of parents

It is often asserted that most parents want oralism. While most hearing parents want their child to speak, this does not necessarily imply a rejection of sign language. Most parents of deaf children are hearing, with little prior knowledge of deafness before having their own child. Information will be largely mediated to them through hearing professionals and they are unlikely to be invited to meet adult Deaf people. If the alternatives are posed in terms of a dichotomy between their child speaking and being part of the hearing world, or signing and being excluded from the hearing world, parents will usually choose the oral approach, particularly if it is offered as a realistic possibility. ◄

3.2 Total Communication

In the 1960s and early 1970s, in response to the failure of deaf education, apparent in research studies such as those of Conrad, there was a move to reinstate signing in the education of deaf children. The last major Government Report on the education of deaf children, the Lewis Report published in 1968, was set up to look at 'the possible place of finger spelling and sign'. While its recommendations were equivocal, it indicates an interest in the topic at this time.

◄ Reading
An account of Total Communication is given in Article 5.6 by Lionel Evans in Reader Two, and you should read this now. ◄

Various signing approaches emerged within the context of Total Communication, largely based on English:

Δ **Sign Supported English:** This has already been described in Unit 3, and is the use of spoken English together with some signs drawn from the lexicon of BSL.

Δ **Signing Exact English:** A number of signing system approaches to education have developed, which comprise signs to represent totally all the elements of the spoken English. Thus additional signs were created to represent various elements that would be expressed differently in BSL; for example, 'ed' and 'ing' endings, 'the', and a sign indicating the possessive ' 's' as in 'woman's coat'. Alongside this, artificial systems were also created—for example, Cued Speech and Paget Gorman Systematic Signing—though these have largely been abandoned now.

Δ **Cued Speech:** This is a system devised by Orin Cornett (a physicist) in an attempt to disambiguate lip patterns. It is recognized that many sounds (e.g. 'p' and 'b' or 'd', 't' and 'n') have the same lip patterns, and the difficulty of lip-reading has been attributed to this. Cornett devised a system of hand movements, near the lips, which would give a different hand pattern for different sounds which had a similar lip pattern. It is not a system of signing in that it is completely subordinate to English.

Figure 5.3 Cued Speech being used
(Source: courtesy of the Royal National Institute for the Deaf)

Δ **Paget Gorman:** Paget Gorman systematic signing system was devised by
a hearing man, Paget, and a deaf man, Gorman. This was an attempt to
make signing, which at that time was seen as a crude gestural system,
more logical and more English. It introduced a hierarchy of categories—
for example, all animals had the sign for animal followed by their own
distinctive sign, and there was an elaborate grammatical system for
marking tense etc.

What is significant about all these signing approaches is that the goal
remains essentially English, and that the signing is only used as a
supplement, and does not represent a recognition of British Sign Language
or of Deaf community and culture. Whilst Total Communication is
presented as a *philosophy* encompassing the full range of communication—
gesture, sign, finger spelling, writing and so on—in practice it is often more
usually interpreted as a *method* of communication in which signs are used
in conjunction with English. As you will appreciate, it is not possible for a
person to speak in English and use British Sign Language at the same time.

Total Communication, interpreted in this narrow way, has received criticism from both the oralists and the Deaf community. Those advocating an oralist approach have published research suggesting that having to sign slows down a teacher's speech, and the language used may be simplified in the attempt to incorporate signs. They have also suggested that it is difficult to attend to signs and speech simultaneously and the message may be confused. In addition, they suggest that the use of signs may discourage children from attending to the speech and thus inhibit spoken language development.

Members of the Deaf community have been more ambivalent in their response to Total Communication. Initially it was welcomed with enthusiasm, as signing was at last to be part of the education of deaf children, and it represented a move away from oralist approaches. You will remember Wendy Daunt on Video Two (Sequence 4) making a comment to this effect. In addition, a Total Communication methodology represented and implied a positive attitude to signing. However, as an approach it is still English based and does not involve British Sign Language. Some Deaf people feel that it does not go far enough and is not working: a slogan that has been used by some Deaf people is 'Total Communication, neither Total nor Communication'. They suggest that BSL is the natural language of Deaf people and therefore the appropriate language for their education.

Overall, Total Communication does not seem to have fulfilled the expectations made of it. In the USA, where it has been used for longer and more widely than in the UK, it has been said:

> Since the 1970s, most deaf students have been educated in Total Communication programs in which some form of signing and speech is used simultaneously for communication and instructional purposes ... most students are still functionally illiterate upon graduation from high school.
>
> (Paul, 1988)

In the short term, however, it seems that the main use of signing in education will be in conjunction with English, although bilingual approaches are beginning to emerge, as will be seen in Section 3.3. However, while the education of deaf children remains dominated by hearing people, English is likely to remain the language used in most school settings. A group of hearing people is unlikely to establish a BSL-using community within a school. But also, most deaf children are born to hearing parents, whose language is likely to be English (the substantial minority where the language of the home is not English is discussed in Section 3.4). Total Communication may reflect more faithfully the language used at home by hearing English-speaking parents. Even if those parents learn to sign, their signing will approximate more to Sign Supported English than to BSL.

3.3 The bilingual option

While the bilingual approach, which advocates the use of BSL and English as separate languages, could be subsumed under the umbrella of Total Communication, it is such a radical shift that we treat it separately here. In endorsing the use of BSL in education, it recognizes Deaf people's language and culture.

◀ Reading

You should now read Article 5.7, 'Bilingualism and the Education of Deaf Children' by Miranda Llwellyn-Jones in Reader Two. ◀

You will note that this reading implies a shift in the goals of education, from preparing deaf children for a hearing society, to allowing deaf children to develop their own cultural identity. This approach is clearly influenced by policies towards other minority languages in the UK, and the recognition that we are a multicultural, multilingual society.

◀ Video

You should watch again the section on the LASER conference on Video Two, Sequence 4, this time to examine the content rather than to observe the interpreting. Note the points made in favour of the bilingual approach. ◀

The bilingual approach to the education of deaf children has been influenced by the use of bilingual education with children from ethnic minority groups who use languages other than English at home. Following the Bullock Report in 1975, which asserted that: 'No child should be expected to cast off the language and culture of the home as he (*sic*) crosses the school threshold, nor to live and act as though school and home represent two totally separate and different cultures which have to be kept firmly apart', there was an increase in interest in mother-tongue teaching in the UK in the late 1970s and early 1980s. In 1978 the Department of Education and Science set up the 'Mother Tongue and English Teaching Project' in several schools in Bradford, and in September 1979 they set up the Linguistic Minorities Project.

During this time there were a number of major programmes introducing minority languages as a medium of education with schools. However, for a number of reasons, the education system has not adopted bilingual methods of education on a large scale. These reasons seem mainly related to the political climate, rather than to research on bilingual education, which yielded results demonstrating that, at very least, it was not detrimental to education and could be positive. The debates around bilingualism in education are fascinating but it is not possible to do justice to them within the scope of this unit.[2]

---

[2] Students wishing to follow these up are recommended to read Cummins and Swain (1986) and the Linguistic Minorities Project (1985). You may also find it useful to consult the Bullock Report (1975) and the Swann Report (1985).

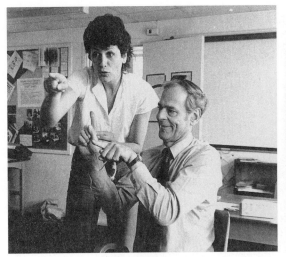

Figure 5.4

Figure 5.5

Figure 5.6

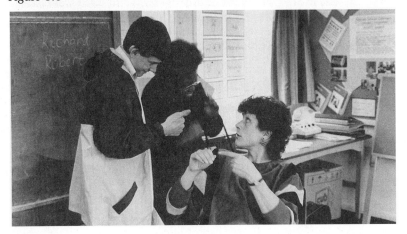

Figure 5.7

Figures 5.4–5.7   Bilingual education in practice in the unit at Derrymount School, Nottingham
(Source: courtesy of Terry Boyle, photographer, and Miranda Pickersgill)

However, the discussions in this area have been instrumental in increasing interest in the possibility of bilingual education for deaf children. The LASER group (part of whose 1989 conference is included on Video Two) was set up in 1983 to 'develop the use of sign language in education'. Among their stated principles are the following:

> 1 BSL has an important role to play in the education of profoundly deaf children, through the necessity of establishing effective communication.
>
> 2 That linguistic competence in BSL can be an important foundation for learning, including the learning of English.
>
> (From LASER Information Booklet, not dated)

Of course, bilingual education with deaf children will be different from bilingual education with children for whom English is not the language of the home, as there will not necessarily be a consistent home language, and children may enter schools with few skills in any language. It is likely that both languages will be largely acquired at school. How programmes will be implemented, how parents will be involved, what the role of Deaf people will be, are all issues currently under discussion.[3]

While the bilingual option is introduced as a new approach here, it should be recognized that some of the great educators of the deaf in the past also saw sign language as integral to the education of deaf people. An excellent account of their work is contained in Harlan Lane's *When the Mind Hears* (Lane, 1988).

◀ Reading
You should now read Article 7.7, 'Deaf People and Minority Groups in the UK' by Jim Kyle in Reader Two, which extends the discussion beyond the school situation. ◀

3.4 The other languages of the United Kingdom

Although the bilingual option has developed in a context of a recognition of a multilingual society, very little consideration has been given to the needs of deaf children for whom English is not the language of the home. A survey by the National Deaf Children's Society (NDCS) in 1986–87 (Speedy, 1987) identified forty-seven home languages other than English in the homes of deaf children. These included British Sign Language and Irish Sign Language. Aside from BSL the most commonly used were Punjabi (all dialects), Urdu and Gujerati.

While there are a number of local initiatives addressing the needs of these families, there is little discussion as to how to recognize deaf children's own

---

[3] These issues are discussed further in two more recent papers by Miranda Llwellyn-Jones (now Pickersgill) which are published in the new journal *Deafness and Development* 'Bi-Lingualism and the Education of Deaf Children: Part 1, Theories, Models and Factors', 1990, vol. 1, no. 1; and 'Bi-Lingualism and the Education of Deaf Children: Part 2, Implications and Practical Considerations', 1990, vol. 1, no. 2.

languages, and thus their culture, within the context of the education of deaf children. The National Deaf Children's Society is the organization which has done most to bring these issues to the fore, and as policy publishes a number of its guides to parents in the main minority languages—Urdu, Cantonese and Punjabi—as well as English.

All too often children from homes where English is not spoken are discussed as 'doubly disadvantaged', and the English-based language policies persist. The families are usually advised to speak English at home if they want the best for their children. At a workshop on the needs of children from ethnic minority groups in 1986, Sajaad Munir, the father of four deaf children, presented a personal viewpoint. The account of the workshop reports that:

> He felt that the late diagnosis of his own 4 children was because their delay in developing language skills was blamed on the different language use in their own home. He described how he and his wife were expected to communicate with their children in English, yet they felt to deprive their children of their mother tongue was a profound loss for them.
>
> (Report on a workshop about the needs of ethnic minority deaf children, Gregory and Meherali, 1986)

Other parents at the workshop endorsed this view.

The response of one of the teachers to the NDCS survey is regrettably unusual: 'There is an exciting variety of home languages spoken here—it makes it a very challenging place to work.'

3.5 The debate over methods

At this point in the unit we would like to bring together the points raised so far.

◄ Reading
You will find it useful here to read Chapters 11 and 12 in the Set Book *Sign Language: The Study of Deaf People and Their Language* by Kyle and Woll. These deal with language and education in the context of the Deaf community. ◄

The current communication practices in the UK can be divided into the following three groups:

Δ   oral approaches

Δ   simultaneous speech and signing

Δ   a bilingual approach based on British Sign Language and English

In order to understand these more thoroughly it is important to distinguish the *language*, English or British Sign Language, from the *mode*, spoken or visual–gestural.

Oral approaches

Language: English

Mode: oral

Simultaneous speech and signing

Language: English (perhaps with
               some BSL features)

Mode: oral and visual–gestural

The bilingual approach

Languages: 1 English

               2 BSL

Mode: 1 oral or visual–gestural
               (i.e. spoken English or
               Sign Supported English)

               2 visual–gestural (BSL)

◄ Activity 4

You should briefly consider and note down the implications of the above approaches for:

(a) the Deaf community;

(b) the involvement of teachers who are themselves deaf;

(c) hearing parents of deaf children;

(d) children from homes where English is not the first language. ◄

In recent years there have been a number of research projects which have attempted to establish that one particular communication form is more effective in the education of deaf children than another. Those advocating signing approaches have argued from the attainments of deaf children of deaf parents. In the 1960s and 1970s several studies were undertaken, and these early studies demonstrated that deaf children of deaf parents did better than deaf children of hearing parents on measures of general attainment, reading, lip-reading and on social development. Some, though not all, studies also showed that these children did better on speech intelligibility (Quigley and Frinsina, 1961; Stuckless and Birch, 1966; Meadow, 1967).

ITQ

Can you suggest possible interpretations of these results?

◄ Comment

Possible factors could be:

(a) early use of sign language in deaf families, so that language competence was established early in the child's life;

(b) deaf parents were more likely to accept the deafness of their children so there was less family stress and thus the children were better adjusted and more able to learn;

(c) there were different causes of deafness in the two groups. For deaf children of deaf parents deafness will be due to genetic factors and is thus unlikely to involve complications. For deaf children of hearing parents the deafness could be due, for example, to rubella, prematurity or meningitis, which could be associated with additional problems leading to lower attainment. ◄

Vernon and Koh (1970) tested the hypothesis that the results were due to different causes of deafness by taking groups of deaf children of deaf and of hearing parents, in which the cause of deafness for all the children was known to be genetic. In fact those children with deaf parents still did better. Most of the early studies attributed the results to the use of sign language in the home. However, as was pointed out in the Unit 3, not all deaf parents use sign language with their children. Corson (1973) compared three groups: deaf children with deaf parents using oral methods; deaf children with deaf parents using signing; and a group of deaf children of hearing parents. Both groups of deaf children of deaf parents did better than those with hearing parents. Corson attributed this to the fact that the deaf parents were more likely to have accepted the deafness than were hearing parents. However, there is an alternative interpretation. As was shown in Unit 3, examining the early development of language in deaf children, deaf parents, regardless of the mode of communication, may be better at establishing basic interaction skills essential for later development.

Other arguments in this debate have centred on the low attainments of deaf children (such as those indicated by Conrad's study), occurring when oralism was the predominant methodology. Those advocating signing have suggested these show the failure of the oral approach. Oralists have replied that oralism has never had a proper test and have asked for evidence for the success of signing methods as used in schools.

In fact the whole issue remains inconclusive. Jensema and Trybus in their major study of communication patterns of 10,509 deaf children in the USA concluded:

> Taken all together, then, the available data suggest that while factors such as the child's hearing level and the family's income level have a large influence on the child's school achievement, variation in communication methods, specifically in the amount of speech used and the amount of sign used, have little relationship with achievement scores, given the existing national variations in the quantity and quality of use of those methods.
>
> (Jensema and Trybus, 1978)

◄ Activity 5

On the basis of what you have read so far, how would you start to develop a policy for the education of deaf children? Write some notes on this before reading further. ◄

◄ Comment
Your own feelings about the method of communication to be used will probably reflect your own ideas about the goals of education for deaf children. You may find it helpful to reflect upon your earlier responses now. ◄

3.6 Learning to communicate or communicating to learn?

The discussion about communication methods in the education of deaf children has taken up a substantial part of this unit. While this reflects the literature on the education of deaf children, we regret that it has been necessary to do this. So much energy goes into this topic, that it is almost as if the education of deaf children is only about language use. We pose the question whether deaf children are 'learning to communicate or communicating to learn?'

The devotion of so much time generally to this issue has had a detrimental effect on other discussion such as how best to teach deaf children to read, to write, to attain mathematically. What are the consequences of various teacher styles in the education of deaf children? We know that deaf children are as cognitively able as hearing children—why then is there not an outcry about their low academic attainments?

These questions have been addressed by the Deaf Research Group at Nottingham University, who have made a detailed analysis of classroom interactions, and attainments in reading and mathematics. However, their major publications to date focus only on children educated in oral settings. They justify this on practical considerations. First, such work depends on detailed analysis which would only be possible with a narrow focus on one method of communication; and second, when they started work, few schools used other than oral approaches. They have recently turned their attention to schools using Sign Supported English approaches.

Many will criticize their exclusive focus on oral settings for the whole range of deaf children, despite the reasons they give, as it may be seen as legitimating the oral approach. However, the strength of their work is that they go beyond the methodology debate to raise critical questions about the education of deaf children. They suggest that raising these questions may also eventually facilitate a more effective evaluation of communication methodology:

> We believe that many arguments about methods of communication have taken place in the absence of sufficient knowledge about the processes of communication that they create. This is reflected in the often polemical and even irrational arguments that all too often characterize talk about 'methods'. By drawing attention to important features of communication and teaching processes we hope to provide new ways of evaluating different methods. In the final chapter, we consider a range of questions and issues that need to be addressed in arguments about methodology. Answers to these, we suggest, will provide more effective ways of deciding whether or not a particular approach to the education of a given child is not working well.
>
> (Wood *et al.*, 1986a)

3.6.1 Reading

Literacy for deaf children is clearly an important skill and thus the teaching of reading warrants particular consideration for the following reasons:

1   For deaf people, reading provides access to the hearing world.

2   Increasingly daily living (work, entertainment, poll tax) requires higher levels of literacy than in the past.

3   Many of the technological developments that could benefit deaf people require reading skills—subtitles on television; minicom and computers.

However, despite the importance of teaching deaf children to read, reading attainments are depressingly low, as was seen in Section 2. Wood *et al.* from the Deaf Research Group of Nottingham University, in their book on the education of deaf children, introduce the chapter on reading by saying, 'This is our gloomiest chapter' (Wood *et al.*, 1986a).

◀ Activity 6

Pause for a moment and consider the process of learning to read for children educated by:

(a) Sign Supported English approaches;

(b) bilingual approaches;

(c) oral approaches. ◀

Not much is known about teaching reading through sign language, although as we indicated earlier, in Section 3.5, there is evidence that deaf children of deaf parents do better. There is a tantalizing finding in the study by Conrad to which we referred in Section 2. Only five of the deafer children (hearing loss greater that 85 db) had a reading level equivalent to the chronological age, but of these, two (40 per cent) had deaf parents. The percentage of deaf children having deaf parents in the population at large is less than 10 per cent. We do not know if in Conrad's sample these were oral deaf parents or signing deaf parents, and we are therefore not able to comment, but it is an interesting finding nevertheless.

3.6.2 Mathematic attainments

A study by Wood and his colleagues suggests that in mathematics, attainments do not show the same extent of lag as do attainments in reading. The results of this study are shown in Table 5.1, and from analysing these results, Wood *et al.* were able to show that:

Δ   The type of provision made makes no difference if hearing loss is taken into account.

Δ   There is some relationship with degrees of hearing loss, but this is not a direct relationship.

Δ Explanations involving language use provide only partial explanation of lag. Teachers overestimated the contribution of language problems to mathematical problems.

Δ Deaf children make similar errors to hearing children, suggesting a *delay* in development rather than *different* development.

Table 5.1 Maths age of deaf pupils in their final year at school (16 years)

Type of school	Hearing loss[4]	Maths age
Special school	92 db	12.1
Partially Hearing Unit	68 db	12.8
Mainstream	48 db	14.0
Hearing children		15.5

(Source: Wood *et al.*, 1986a)

Studies by others have shown that:

Δ In computer-assisted teaching in mathematics deaf children showed greater gains than hearing children of the same age (Suppes, 1974).

Δ In France, a group of teachers are developing a system of teaching mathematics by demonstrating, directly through mathematical symbols, which does not require conventional language (spoken or sign).

ITQ
What might be the implications of these findings?

Wood *et al.* conclude:

> In conclusion, we suggest that the time is right to consider whether, particularly in the later years of schooling, our concern for the linguistic development of children leads us to underestimate and undervalue their potential and needs in other areas of the curriculum. Indeed, it may well be the case that linguistic development itself would be better served by *using* language to teach and instruct in such subjects as mathematics.

(Wood *et al.*, 1986a)

[4] Degrees of hearing loss are discussed in Section 4.2.

3.6.3 Teaching style

Wood and his colleagues have also looked at classroom interaction in both oral and signing settings. They find that the teaching style employed has implications for the participation of the pupils.

◀ Reading
You should now look at Article 5.8, 'Teaching and Talking with Deaf Children' by David Wood, Heather Wood, Amanda Griffiths and Ian Howarth in Reader Two. ◀

This particular reading is based on studies in schools using oral methods. More recently Wood and colleagues have used the same approach in schools using Sign Supported English and they conclude:

> We found no evidence that the frequency with which teachers accompanied their words with sign had any impact either on their style of interaction or upon our measures of the performance of children in conversation. Frequency of signing was not associated with less teacher control or with less frequent repair. There was some evidence that, as a group, the teachers here displayed a lower incidence of complex clause structure in their speech than teachers using oral methods. And like the oral teachers, there was no increase in complexity of speech with age as happens with hearing children. These findings imply that the use of signing does not 'liberate' teachers by leading them to adopt a more relaxed, less controlling style of interaction or to produce grammatically more complex language, questions which motivated some of our analyses. Indeed it may be the case that the cognitive demands placed on teachers by the need to sign as they speak inhibits the production of embedded clause structures in their speech, although we can only speculate about the factors which influence the grammatical register of teacher speech. At the same time, we found no evidence to support the hypothesis that the use of signs by teachers led to any frequent or regular breakdown of grammatical coherence in their utterances.
>
> (Wood *et al.*, submitted for publication)

It is, however, the practical application of their research that may be the more interesting. It was found that teachers could adjust their style of interaction with consequences for the quality of the interaction. It may be that alerting teachers to aspects of conversational style may facilitate better communication.

4 The education of deaf children: disabled group or linguistic minority?

Before going on to look at the second issue raised by deaf people in the accounts of their education (that of integration), we will consider the context of education, and the model of deafness that informs the educational processes.

◀ Activity 7

From your reading of the course so far, to what extent do you feel deaf children are seen within education as disabled or as members of a linguistic minority group? Make a few notes on this before you continue. ◀

◀ Comment

While the bilingual approach seems to recognize the cultural significance of deafness, the other approaches seem to see deafness as implying a deficiency to be made good. ◀

4.1 Terminology and the education of deaf children

To consider fully the question posed in Activity 7 we must examine educational terminology. In Units 2 and 3 the word 'deaf' was used in an unproblematic way. However, within education, pupils are generally referred to as 'hearing-impaired'. The local authority organization responsible is usually called 'Services for the Hearing-Impaired', although, interestingly, teachers remain 'teachers of the deaf', and schools, 'schools for the deaf'. The term 'hearing-impaired' was first introduced in the USA. Originally it seems to have been used for children with lesser hearing losses, who could benefit from aids and function as hearing people. Gradually its use appears to have been appropriated to cover all pupils, whatever the hearing loss.

The use of the terms 'deaf' and 'hearing-impaired' are often confused. The 'Report of the Committee of Enquiry into the Education of Handicapped Children and Young People', more often known as 'The Warnock Report' (1978) and the precursor of the 1981 Education Act, has the following statements on two adjacent pages:

> 7.49 Moreover integration in an ordinary school might be impracticable for children with **impaired** hearing if the school was adjacent to a main road.

> 7.51—whilst **deaf** children must not be at risk through inability to hear personal instruction or warning sounds.
>
> (Warnock Report, 1978; our emphasis)

However, the choice of terminology does have implications for the way in which educational provision is discussed. The British Association of Teachers of the Deaf (BATOD) specifies that children with a hearing loss should be referred to as 'hearing-impaired' and explicitly states that, 'the terms "deaf" and "partially hearing" should no longer be used to describe the hearing status of hearing-impaired children' (BATOD, Article 5.1 in Reader Two). Tucker and Nolan of the Manchester University Department of Audiology and Education of the Deaf, which has been responsible for the training of most teachers of the deaf in this country, refer to 'hearing-impaired' as the less stigmatizing term (Tucker and Nolan, 1984).

However, as Padden and Humphries point out in talking about the USA, but it could equally apply to the UK:

> Although in recent years the term 'hearing impaired' has been proposed by many in an attempt to include both deaf people and other people who do not hear, deaf people still refer to themselves as DEAF.
>
> (Padden and Humphries, 1988)

ITQ
What are the different implications of the terms 'deaf' and 'hearing-impaired'?

◀ Comment
The term 'deaf' can be seen to imply a positive cultural identity. 'Hearing-impaired' implies a deficiency with respect to hearing people, and thus the emphasis is on cure and remediation, rather than on a recognition of deafness in itself, and on the existence of a separate Deaf community and culture. ◀

4.2 The impact of audiology

Beyond the actual terms 'deaf' or 'hearing-impaired', also significant are those factors which educationalists find critical. These include:

Δ   degree of hearing loss

Δ   type of hearing loss

Δ   age of onset of hearing loss

Δ   aeteology of hearing loss

Article 5.1 'Audiological Descriptors' by the British Association of Teachers of the Deaf, in Reader Two, gives an account of the classification of the degree of hearing loss.

That the classification of the degree of hearing loss is an issue for educationalists is clear from the fact that most books on the education of deaf children start by describing the categories of hearing loss (cf. Moores, 1978; Quigley and Kretschmer, 1982).

While all these factors are not seen as relevant to the Deaf community, they have acquired relevance in education and this itself is of importance. The Deaf community distinguishes between deaf people in terms of their identification with the Deaf community and with Deaf culture ('deaf' and 'Deaf' as discussed in Unit 1), but find the educational categories irrelevant and do not describe themselves, or distinguish among themselves, in this way. In recent separate research studies interviewing young deaf people and deaf teachers, questions about degree of hearing loss have usually been dismissed as irrelevant by the majority of those interviewed (Silo, work in progress; Gregory *et al.*, work in progress). When categories have been given, attention has been drawn to the fact that these have been externally imposed: '*they say* I'm profoundly deaf' or '*I've been told* I'm moderately deaf'.

Regardless of the usefulness of the categories to educationalists, though, it is important to consider their consequences. There is an implication that different sorts of remediation are appropriate at different levels of hearing loss, for different causes, or for different ages of onset. It is also clear that many more children are under the remit of the education authority than will go on to be members of the Deaf community, as educators consider the whole range of children with differing degrees of deafness.

The underpinning of deaf education by a notion of hearing impairment itself has wide-reaching implications. Deaf children are seen as impaired and deficient, and lacking normal hearing. Thus the job of the teacher is constructed as one of restoring loss, remediating, and making good what is lacking. This creates a context in which the expectations of deaf pupils are low and is implicit in much writing about the education of deaf children.

4.3 The impact of technology

Earlier it was suggested that one of the reasons for the persistence of oralism was the promise of technology and technological advances—that improvements in hearing aids would make it possible for all children with a hearing loss, no matter what the degree, to benefit from an oral education. Such total optimism for hearing aids now seems misplaced, and for the foreseeable future there will be a significant group of children for whom this is an unrealistic prospect.

One of the problems of conventional hearing aids has been that they amplify everything, including all the background noise. Hearing people can use their hearing selectively and, in effect, blot out sounds to which they do not wish to attend. Conventional hearing aids do not do this and the sound of the voice can be lost against the background of a noisy room.

Radio aids go some way to eliminating the problem. The deaf child wears a radio receiver and the teacher wears a transmitter, comprising a microphone and transmitter antennae. This cuts out background sounds. Usually the aid acts as a conventional aid as well; it is not always the case that the child needs to hear the teacher, but may want to attend to other things. The deaf child has to learn to manage the radio aid, switching between the two possible modes. Despite the sophistication of such aids, however, even the best can only amplify those frequencies in which the child already has

Figure 5.8 Hearing aids in use
(Source: courtesy of the Royal School for the Deaf, Derby)

some hearing. Hearing aids do not restore perfect hearing in the way that spectacles can restore vision. Many deaf adults reject hearing aids completely as being of no practical use.

It is clear that the technological developments have made it possible for an increasing number of children to use spoken language as the medium of education. Unfortunately, such changes have focused attention on the remediation of hearing loss, to the detriment of those children for whom hearing aids are of limited help in providing access to spoken language, and for whom new and different approaches to education are required. It has been a recurring theme in this unit that, because services for hearing-impaired children deal with a whole range of hearing loss, procedures relevant for some children have been adopted inappropriately for others. A major focus on audiological procedures, measurement of hearing loss, and remediation by hearing aids, has deflected attention from situations which need different consideration.

5 Integration

5.1 Educational provision for deaf children

The 1981 Education Act shifted the emphasis from specific categories of disabled pupils (e.g. deaf and partially hearing) to pupils with 'special needs'. However, the categories of educational provision (schools for the deaf, Partially Hearing Units) retain the distinctions made in the 1944 Education Act. (See the *Legislation Booklet* for further details of these Acts.) These were clarified and defined by the Ministry of Education in 1962 as:

> deaf pupils: that is to say, pupils with impaired hearing who require education by methods suitable for pupils with little or no naturally acquired speech or language.

> partially hearing pupils: that is to say, pupils with impaired hearing whose development of speech and language, even if retarded, is following a normal pattern, and who require for their education special arrangements or facilities, though not necessarily all the educational methods used for deaf children.
>
> (Ministry of Education Circular 10/62, 1962)

Specialist education for deaf children is thus provided in:

△ **Schools for the deaf**: Some of these are day schools only, some are for day pupils and boarders (weekly, half-termly and termly).

△ **Schools for the partially hearing**: As above, these could be day schools only or cater for boarding pupils as well.

△ **Units for the partially hearing**: These are classes attached to mainstream schools and each class has a specialist teacher plus an assistant and four to ten pupils. Units usually consist of one class, but there can be more.

As well as specialist provision, there have always been deaf children in mainstream education. However, it should not necessarily be assumed that schools for the deaf, schools for the partially hearing, and units differ along the lines implied by the definitions, either in their teaching methods or in the population of children for whom they cater. The allocation of children to schools, units or mainstream education largely relates to the policy of particular local education authorities (LEAs). Lynas (1984) compared four local education authorities in England and looked at the placement of children aged 5–16 years with an average hearing loss of 70 db and above. Her results are indicated in Table 5.2.

Table 5.2 The educational placement of deaf pupils in four LEAs in England

LEA	Special school for the hearing impaired	Unit	Individual placement in ordinary school	Total
A	28 (82%)	—	6 (18%)	34
B	7 (28%)	18 (72%)	—	25
C	10 (26%)	23 (61%)	5 (13%)	38
D	13 (33%)	14 (34%)	13 (33%)	40

(Source: Lynas, 1984)

While the schools and units, in their titles, still refer to deaf and partially hearing, this terminology has been superseded with respect to the pupils. The 1981 Education Act implemented in 1983 brought in the global category of 'special educational needs' to describe a child who 'has a learning difficulty which calls for special educational provision to be made for him (*sic*)'. While it was recognized that, for convenience, descriptive terms will be needed for particular groups of children who receive special educational provision, and deaf children are included in that, the Warnock Report (on which the 1981 Education Act was based) recommended that the statutory categorization of handicapped pupils be abolished.

The impact of the 1981 Education Act was not only in its concept of 'special needs', but in its aim that, wherever possible, any child with special needs should be educated in an ordinary, rather than a special school. The Act states that it is the duty of the local authority to ensure that a child is educated in an ordinary school provided:

1   He or she receives any special provision required.
2   The special provision is compatible with education being provided for the other children.
3   There is sufficiency of resources.

Before the Act, taking into account all children with a hearing loss, most were educated in mainstream schools. However, increasingly, local education authorities are adopting a policy of integrating all children with special needs. While this may seem to be a consequence of the Act, in fact changes began before this, and the Act reflected, as well as influenced, practice. The gradual increase in the number of children with a hearing loss in integrated settings may not be significant in absolute terms; there are indicators, however, that more children with greater hearing losses are now educated in mainstream schools.

5.2 The impact of integration policies

From your reading at the beginning of this unit, you will have found that many Deaf people are opposed to integration.

◄ Activity 8

Make notes for yourself on the arguments that could be advanced for and against the integration of deaf children.

When you have completed this from your own perspective, consider the different arguments that could be advanced by:

(a) the Deaf community;

(b) a deaf child;

(c) hearing parents of a deaf child;

(d) teachers of the deaf;

(e) teachers in the mainstream setting with deaf children in the classes. ◄

◄ Comment

In putting down your thoughts you may have needed to ask, which deaf children? If you considered those deaf children growing up to be part of the Deaf community, you may have felt differently from the way you would if you were considering all children with a hearing loss. You may also have asked whether there would be the following in the integrated setting:

Δ   specialist support

Δ   an interpreter, for while integration is often seen as going hand-in-hand with oralist approaches to education, this does not have to be the case. ◄

The 1981 Education Act has been seen as a means of denying deaf children access to the Deaf community. The implication of sending all children to their local school is that any deaf child is likely to be the only one in their class. In a recent interview study a deaf young woman, herself in favour of an integrated system of education, spoke of this problem:

> I think we are losing contact with [deaf] people in mainstreaming because they become 'hearing' again. They are 'pretending' to be hearing—I don't know whether they do that or not. But I know we are losing contact with deaf children, which I think is very sad because they have got to have some kind of centre to fall back on and if you go to the deaf club you can relax because you are with people who are the same as you—got something in common.
> (Deaf woman, 22 years, educated in mainstream school and a boarding school for the deaf. From an interview conducted in spoken English, in Gregory *et al.*, work in progress)

Some groups within the Deaf community itself have seen integration as an attack on the Deaf community and Deaf culture. Over recent years a number of schools for the deaf have closed, although this is probably due as much to falling numbers with the school-age population in general and to falling numbers of deaf children, as to the policy of placing deaf children in their local schools. The National Union of the Deaf (NUD) has argued favourably that integration is a way of destroying the Deaf community:

Another example of the growing influence of the Protectors[5] can be seen in the current moves towards so-called integration. This is resulting in the closure of five deaf schools, and the placing of deaf children in hearing schools despite the fact that deaf people are unanimously opposed to this. The trend towards integration constitutes nothing less than genocide[6] and this matter is dealt with separately here. Deaf people feel that some integration can only be achieved when hearing children and adults learn the sign language where appropriate. The results of a policy of assimilation are to split up the deaf community to the extent where it can no longer make its objections heard, and thus another example of the Protectors removing any threat to their powers of advocacy.

(National Union of the Deaf, circa 1982)

Integration of deaf children has also been portrayed as a way of perpetuating oralism. The integration–segregation argument often sounds like the old oral–manual debate. While it is the case that integrating deaf children means it is likely they will be educated through speech, the two issues should not be confused. Integration can take place within a context of sign language in education by the use of interpreters. This is common practice in the USA and is an approach that is being pioneered at this moment in Leeds.

Yet whatever we may feel about integration and its consequences for deaf children, it is important to be clear about the reasons why it has come about. While one way of viewing integration is as a move to destroy the Deaf community, another view is to see the 1981 Education Act in the context of changing attitudes towards disabled people in general, in the UK and throughout the Western World. (Within legislation deaf people are classified as disabled, and this is discussed further in Unit 8.) The policy of integration is not just directed at deaf children but at all children with disabilities. It arose from the legitimate concern that whole groups of children were being marginalized inappropriately and were not being prepared for an 'ordinary' life. This trend towards the integration of deaf children is part of a general move towards the placement of children with special needs into mainstream education and reflects the changing attitude to disability in general. What integration means to many disabled people is aptly expressed in a report on disability published in the UK in 1976:

> Integration for the disabled means a thousand things. It means the absence of segregation. It means social acceptance. It means being able to be treated like everybody else. It means the right to work, to go to cinemas, to enjoy outdoor sport, to have a family life and a social life and a love life, to contribute materially to the community, to have the usual choices of association, movement and activity, to go on holiday to the usual places, to be educated up to university level with one's unhandicapped peers, to travel without fuss on public transport.
>
> (Snowdon Working Party, 1976)

---

[5] 'Protectors' are defined in the report as 'those who have taken positions of power in the education of deaf children, who wish to impose a different belief on the deaf community'.

[6] Genocide is defined in the report from the United Nations' Convention on Prevention and Punishment of the Crime of Genocide as 'any of the following acts committed with intent to destroy a whole, or in part a national, racial, ethnic or religious group as such'.

5.3 The goals of integration

Integration itself is generally seen as fulfilling two main purposes:

1 The fostering of social integration such that the child is educated alongside his or her peers and is not isolated from them.

2 Access to a wider curriculum than in special schools, which have been seen as often offering a restricted curriculum because of their smaller size, and also because the teachers are often specialists in the particular needs of their pupils, rather than in the subjects under tuition.

ITQ

To what extent could integrating deaf children answer those needs? You could reflect upon how your answer to this ITQ relates to the comments you made in Activity 5 on the goals of education for deaf children.

For deaf children the issue of social integration raises the question of who the peers of deaf children are—are they deaf or hearing children? Your answer to the ITQ above may have reflected your views on this. It also raises the question as to whether deaf children should perhaps be integrated into both the Deaf and hearing communities.

The curriculum of specialist education for deaf children has often focused on language learning. What would access to a wider curriculum therefore entail for a deaf child? The existence of a wider curriculum does not necessarily imply that all of it is available to the deaf child. We raise further questions about this issue in Section 5.5.

5.4 Studies of integration

Attitudes to integration reflect more general attitudes to education. In this section we will consider three major papers on the integration of deaf children, all of which are included in Reader Two.

One of the major studies undertaken in this country has been that of Lynas (1986a). Lynas used participant observations and interviews in mainstream settings and units, and with deaf children at a range of different ages. She also interviewed classroom teachers and other hearing children in the schools.

She concludes:

> My research findings indicate that an education in an ordinary school is popular with hearing-impaired pupils and young people.

On the social side she says:

> The evidence from my research revealed that pupils with a hearing handicap were generally accepted into the social milieu of *normally hearing* pupils and were treated in a friendly manner and indeed in many instances were 'made friends with'. In nearly all mainstream classes there were *normally hearing* pupils prepared to offer helpful accommodation and constructive support to a deaf classmate in order to facilitate his (*sic*) understanding of lessons.

And on the development of speech:

> All the hearing impaired pupils and young people subscribed to the principle of normalization in that they all believed the major goal in deaf education should be teaching deaf children to talk. They believed that the ordinary school, in providing a *normal spoken language* environment, offered them as deaf pupils the best available means of acquiring the ability to talk normally.
>
> (Lynas, 1986a, our emphasis)

 ◀ Reading
You should now read Article 5.9, 'Integrating the Handicapped into Ordinary Schools' by Wendy Lynas in Reader Two. ◀

Lynas' study has been subjected to a great deal of criticism (Gregory, 1987; Booth, 1988; Arnold, 1988). Some of the criticisms may have been apparent from reading the short quotations above. Lynas' emphasis is on education as normalization—that is, that the goal of education is to enable all pupils to be as 'normal' (i.e. like everyone else) as possible, and that the development of spoken language is part of this. The use of the word 'normal' every time 'hearing' is used implies that 'not hearing' is 'abnormal' and this speaks volumes in terms of attitude.

There is also a patronizing attitude to the deaf pupils, an example of which can be found in the second of the three quotations above, in the statement about how the hearing pupils would help those who were deaf. Gregory comments further on this in her review:

> Lynas appears to think that the misunderstandings of the deaf child may endear her/him to classmates. A particular example she gives concerns a deaf child who was asked to find a parallelogram. After searching he returned to ask the shape of a pelican. She says 'this misunderstanding caused pleasurable laughter when recounted to the whole class and in a sense enhanced his acceptability within the class' (p. 105). The question to be asked is what constitutes this acceptability, as a child who is an integrated member of the class, or as the class joker. I am also rather taken aback at the acceptance of patronising attitudes on the part of the teachers and pupils to the deaf pupils, such as 'She's got a delightful sunny way'. 'She's so gentle and smiling all the time' (p. 92). Lynas develops this theme by saying:

'The research suggests, therefore, that if a deaf child has particularly pleasing qualities or special abilities his integration into the ordinary class will be facilitated. An implication of this finding is that those responsible for the education of deaf children should take every possible step to develop any talents or good personal qualities that a deaf child may possess.' (p. 93). Does this really mean that what we want for deaf children is acceptance on the basis of their endearing characteristics rather than an education based on their needs?

(Gregory, 1987)

Lynas asserts in her study that all the hearing-impaired pupils favoured integration, but both Gregory and Booth point out that a close reading of Lynas' book provides ample evidence to the contrary:

Alison, 12 years: They keep making fun of me. They say 'you're deaf' and they go 'aah, aah, aah ...' and I don't like it, it's horrible.

James, 17 years: I came home from school and cried every single night.

(Lynas, 1986a)

And these are only two of the many examples that could have been chosen.

Perhaps it was the style of questioning that elicited so many answers in approval of integration. While the actual questions asked are not reported, the use of the word 'normal' to mean 'not deaf' and statements such as 'most deaf pupils and young people do not want to be part of a distinctive and exclusive deaf subculture' indicate the form the questions may have taken.

Certainly other studies do not find this overwhelming support for integration. Arnold reports the study by Harvey in which the results were far more complex. Sixty per cent of those deaf people interviewed had experienced integrated and special education, and, while only 14 per cent were unhappy with their experiences, would send their own deaf children to special schools. He says:

What emerges from Harvey's study is the variety and complexity of the attitudes of deaf people. They are not a homogeneous population as regards their attitudes to their own education and their feelings about integration at home and in adult life.

(Arnold, 1988)

◀ Reading
You should now read Article 5.10, 'Challenging Conceptions of Integration' by Tony Booth in Reader Two. ◀

Booth provides an interesting analysis of Lynas. He himself is a staunch advocate of integration, and his challenge is to Lynas' notion of normalization rather than to the ideology of integration. For him integration is a celebration of diversity, with the onus on school and teachers to meet fully the adverse educational needs of their pupils, rather than on the pupils to conform as far as possible to a rigid school system.

While accepting that deaf people are a linguistic minority, he feels that provision for this minority, as for others, should be within the context of mainstream education. For him, treating deaf children as a linguistic minority does not imply that they should be educated in special schools.

◄ Reading
You should now read Article 5.11, 'The Mainstreaming of Primary Age Deaf Children' by Susan Gregory and Juliet Bishop in Reader Two. ◄

The study by Gregory and Bishop is different in emphasis. Rather than looking at the satisfaction or dissatisfaction with integration, it examines in detail whether integration for deaf children meets its goals.

The approach of this study is to examine the process of integration itself, by seeing what happens in the classroom. One of the main moves towards integrated education in general was the result of a dissatisfaction with some special schools which were seen as having a limited syllabus and not providing the range of opportunities and the full curriculum available in mainstream schools. Integration has also been seen as a way of exposing deaf children to spoken language:

> Integration is therefore seen as an integral part of a natural auditory approach to the development of spoken language in hearing impaired children as well as a means of exposing the child to normal levels of academic and social achievement.

> (Harrison, 1986)

This notion, that placing deaf children in the mainstream classroom automatically exposes them to the normal curriculum, is challenged in the article by Gregory and Bishop. They argue that individual integration as currently practised does not give the child access to the curriculum, as the child cannot participate fully, and moreover, the deaf child develops coping strategies which are counter-productive to the goals of education.

5.5 The future for the education of deaf children

At the time of writing (June, 1990) the future for the education of deaf children remains unclear. The Education Reform Act of 1988 (see the *Legislation Booklet* for further details) is likely to bring about far-reaching changes but it is difficult to ascertain what these will be. Two areas of the Act, in particular, seem of major significance: the National Curriculum and the financial delegation to schools.

The National Curriculum, whereby all children will be tested on core curriculum subjects four times during their school careers, raises the following questions with regard to deaf pupils:

△ To what extent will deaf pupils be involved in the National Curriculum, as pupils with special educational needs can be excluded from it or can have it modified to meet their needs?

△ Will the expectations of those pupils who are excluded be lower and the expectations of the teachers decline?

△ What will be the place of BSL in a curriculum designed with hearing children in mind?

The financial delegation to schools means that schools (apart from primary schools with less than 200 pupils) will be given responsibility for their own budgets. It is not clear what impact this will have on those children with special needs for whom additional requirements are appropriate.

6 Deaf people and the education of deaf children

In the discussion of both these debates on language and communication, and on integration, what has been missing has been the perspective of Deaf people themselves. It seems to have been assumed that Deaf people have nothing useful to say about the education of deaf children. It has also been assumed that they have nothing useful to contribute in the educational process, in that until recently they have been effectively banned from posts within the educational system.

6.1 Organizations of Deaf people

In fact, while the opinions of Deaf people may not have been taken into account, they have always been stated. The largest organization of Deaf people in the UK, the British Deaf Association (BDA) was founded in 1890 as a direct consequence of the Milan Conference and the subsequent Royal Commission of 1889 in the UK which endorsed the decisions of that conference. An excellent history of the BDA, including an account of its role in education, is given in Brian Grant's book *The Deaf Advance: A History of the British Deaf Association 1890–1990.*

In January 1890 a meeting was called in London of Adult Deaf and Dumb Missions and Associations. The following resolution was proposed:

> That this conference is of the opinion that the combined system,[7] as advocated by Dr. E.M. Gallaudet, before the Royal Commission, is calculated to confer the greatest benefit upon the greatest number of deaf and dumb (*sic*).

[7] 'Combined system' refers to a communication of signing, finger spelling and speech.

The motion was passed by twenty-one to three, and led to the founding of the British Deaf and Dumb Association (BDDA), now the BDA. The BDA has always recommended the use of sign language within the education of deaf children, and has at various times engaged in dialogues with teachers of the deaf. The Association also submitted proposals to the various congresses on the education of the deaf, following Milan, including a detailed one to the Liege conference of 1905. Discussions were also maintained with the National Association of Teachers of the Deaf. It is interesting to note that the proposal, for one such meeting in 1907, to establish better working relationships, suggested that 'discussions on methods were to be avoided'. The BDDA accepted this, providing 'the schools understood that they as an Association did not give up one iota of the opinions, which they have always held concerning the system adopted in the deaf' (quotation from the minutes of the 1907 meeting). The current education policy of the BDA maintains the same view that deaf children should have access to sign language.

In 1976 the National Union of the Deaf was founded as an organization 'run by Deaf people, for Deaf people'. It has campaigned strenuously for the introduction of sign language into the education of deaf children, and against integration. In a strongly worded report to the United Nations (not dated, circa 1982) the NUD comments:

> 1 That British Sign Language be accepted officially as a native language of the UK, as has Swedish Sign Language been accepted in Sweden.
>
> 2 That it is recognised that Sign Languages should be the vehicle of education of the profoundly deaf child in the UK, who should be educated bi-lingually in English and British Sign Language.
>
> 3 That the deaf community of the UK is a linguistic/ethnic minority of that country, and as such to be regarded as under the protection of the UN's International Covenant on Political and Civil Rights.
>
> 4 That under Article 27, the Convention on the Prevention and Punishment of the Crime of Genocide be recognised as applying to the BSL using linguistic community of the UK.
>
> 5 Following the recognition of recommendation 1, that it become officially established by the British Government that the deaf child should be taught in their native tongue first, and that English should be taught alongside this simultaneously so that they can become bilingual.
>
> 6 Following recommendation 4, any attempt to prevent the UK Government carrying out of this, or failure to implement fully, is recognised as a crime of genocide under Article 2 of the UN Convention.
>
> 7 That, although the case for genocide in retrospect is strong, the perpetrators of it be not considered for eligibility before the International Court of Human Rights.

Part of the NUD's argument against integration was quoted in Section 5.2.

6.2 Deaf people working within the education system

In Section 3.5, which looked at the various approaches to language to be used with deaf children, you were asked to consider the implications of the various approaches for the employment of teachers who are themselves deaf. There would seem to be no role for Deaf teachers in an oral system, although it could be (and has been argued) that teachers who are themselves deaf have special knowledge which could help children understand and develop speech. Also, until recently, the few deaf people who became teachers were those with oral skills. Deaf teachers could have a role in sign-supported approaches, although as these approaches are English based, the teachers would also have to be fluent in the use of English. The clearest role is in the bilingual approach, and to establish a fully bilingual environment, Deaf teachers are essential.

However, currently there is no real access to the profession of teacher of the deaf for deaf people unless they have good oral skills; years of an oral approach have meant that deaf teachers have been largely excluded from the education of deaf children. Although this exclusion has never been total, and there have always been a few deaf teachers, since 1900 these could be numbered in tens rather than hundreds (Silo, work in progress).

ITQ

What are the implications of a system of educating deaf children in which there are virtually no deaf teachers?

◀ Comment

(a) Teachers are educating pupils for failure, in that they do not believe the pupils are able to become teachers. Mary Hare, an oral grammar school for deaf children in this country, while running series of talks on careers, does not include one on being a teacher (ex-pupil, personal communication).

(b) The lack of role models and the identification of deaf people in subordinate positions: hearing people teach, deaf pupils learn. A significant number of deaf children, because they have never encountered a deaf adult, believe that they themselves will grow up to be hearing, as was seen in Unit 2. ◀

Prior to the Milan Conference, many deaf people were involved in the education of deaf children. So much was this taken for granted that the records of the institutions do not specify whether the assistants are deaf or hearing and detailed research is necessary to establish this (Silo, work in progress).

Certainly it seems that after the Milan Conference, many deaf teachers were sacked (as mentioned in Section 3.1.1). Moreover, the fading art of the pupil–teacher system, a procedure by which pupils stayed on at school for extra years to act as teachers, meant that the possibility of extra deaf teachers was denied.

Figure 5.9

Figure 5.10

Figures 5.9 and 5.10   A Deaf man working in the classroom at Derrymount School, Nottingham
(Source: courtesy of Terry Boyle, photographer, and Miranda Pickersgill)

It has proved difficult for deaf people to become teachers. The medical requirement that a teacher can hear a voice at 25 yards is one hurdle, although this has been interpreted in different ways (e.g. can *communicate* at 25 yards). The new requirement that all teachers of the deaf must have experience in a hearing school may prove to be yet another barrier.

◀ Reading
You should now re-read Article 19, 'A Deaf Teacher: A Personal Odyssey' by Janice Silo in Reader One. There are also comments from Janice on Video Two, Sequence 4. In addition, you may like to review Article 10 by Paddy Ladd. ◀

It seems that the barriers to deaf people becoming teachers are not only the legal ones, or issues around the teaching of hearing pupils, but attitudinal ones, particularly from other staff members. You may have found the different attitudes of teachers of the deaf and teachers of the hearing, surprising. There are now signs of change, albeit small ones. LASER has been a growing pressure group for the use of sign language in the education of deaf children, and the employment of deaf teachers. A few schools for the deaf and a few local authorities are seeking to recruit deaf people, and implementation of a bilingual policy in some schools makes this necessary. Interpreter support is now provided for a handful of deaf people wishing to train as teachers. The licensed teacher system, which will side-step the requirements for teaching in ordinary schools, may provide a route into the profession. Deaf teachers have organized themselves into a support group, through which they can support each other. The crèche at the LASER conference (Video Two, Sequence 5) was staffed by deaf students training to be nursery nurses at the only specialist course of its kind at Basford College, Nottingham.

ITQ
What problems do you envisage in including deaf people in education after a long period of exclusion?

There are a number of issues that you might identify here. Deaf people's own experience of the education system, in which they have been oppressed and made to feel inadequate, may mitigate against them feeling comfortable in the role of teacher. Teachers of the deaf themselves have often had a relationship with deaf people that has only involved deaf children and they may find it difficult to see deaf people as partners. Janice Silo has also pointed out that there could be a clash of cultures for deaf people, that the expectations of the Deaf community may clash with those of the education system (Jones, formerly Silo, 1985).

7 The parents' view

7.1 Hearing parents

A further viewpoint which must be important is that of the parents and families. Most parents, more than 90 per cent, will be hearing and will have little or no experience of deafness prior to the birth of their child.

◄ Activity 9
Consider the issues that face hearing parents of deaf children. You may find it useful to review the parents' views in Reader One, in Articles 4, 5, 6 and 7 by Kathy Robinson, Riki Kittel, Heather MacDonald and Lorraine Fletcher, respectively. ◄

The decisions that face parents involve the method of communication to use at home, and the sort of educational provision they wish for their children. As is clear from the Reader articles you have just read, the information given to parents, on which they can base their decisions, may be limited or one-sided. However, given all possible information, the range of choices may still represent a dilemma for them—for example, the oralists will suggest that spoken language is possible and produce children who demonstrate this—and involve a great deal of time and effort on their part.

Figure 5.11   Mother with her deaf child
(Source: courtesy of the Royal National Institute for the Deaf)

Implicit in the choice for the parents is, on the one hand, the acceptance that their child is 'disabled', and that their aim should be remediation to enable the child to be as 'normal' as possible. The alternative would be the introduction of sign language. Implicit in this, on the other hand, is the acceptance that their child may grow up to be part of the Deaf community, a linguistic minority group, which, in turn, implies the recognition that their child is different in some way.

The following quotations from mothers of deaf children indicate the complexity of some of the decisions involved.

A mother, interviewed when her daughter was twenty:

Interviewer: Did the school at that time convey any strong ideas about the way you should communicate?
Mother: Yes. Just with speech.
Interviewer: How did you feel about that at the time?
Mother: At the time you are actually very grieved and it sounded very sensible at the time. You are living in a normal world, therefore you should communicate in a normal way as everybody else does and make it easier for the normal way of going on. It seemed reasonable at the time.

Later, this mother decided that oral approaches were not working with her daughter and learnt to use signs. Another mother of a grown-up daughter illustrates the complexity of the issues:

Interviewer: What in particular was your biggest concern?
Mother: Well, that people would understand her. You see this is why I was so against sign language in the beginning. I was so terrified. I was absolutely terrified that if she learnt sign language right from the word go, as a very young child, that that would be her only form of communication, you see, with her being profoundly deaf I felt if she once gets into this sign language, into the swing of it, that would be her only form of communication. Now, as horrible as this sounds, she is in the minority and she has to go out into a hearing world and everybody is not going to learn sign language for Isabel,[8] you see. So I felt she must learn to communicate with hearing people as best she can on their level. As horrible as that might sound. But it is a sad fact of life, I am afraid, because people have not got the patience with deafness that they have with blindness, or any other handicap as far as that goes. I mean people quickly lose patience with deaf people. I know it is horrible but it is a fact.
Interviewer: So you are really quite glad, nevertheless, that you pursued the oral approach?
Mother: Yes. I am but I think the idyllic situation would be Total Communication if it is possible.
Interviewer: Do you use any signs yourself?
Mother: No. Because Isabel does not want me to sign.
Interviewer: That is interesting. Why … has she said?

[8] Name changed to respect confidentiality.

Mother: I know why it is. Because she is so terrified if I sign she will lose what speech she has got, so while she is at home she has to speak. Now if her Dad and I and her sister use sign language ... I think that is what she is terrified of ... that she would lose ... So, she has always said, 'No, I don't want any of you to sign'.

Here, another mother talks about integration and the reason why she eventually favoured special schooling for her child, at least in the early stages, although she sees this as having disadvantages later on:

Mother: If I had been offered normal education for my children when they were young I would have jumped at it because the thing most parents want is to think there isn't a problem and that they can fit into a normal going on. Really what you want is normality! All right, you might want a very intelligent child, but basically you want a normal intelligent child that will fit into the general pattern. Every parent does and I don't care what you say, that is really what they want! If someone had come along to me and said, 'Yes, deaf children can manage perfectly well in normal school', I would not have been aware, and it would have taken years to become aware, of the problems that that was going to mean for them in future. All sorts of things! Even with specialist help.

Interviewer: Do you think the Unit [Partially Hearing Unit] could have worked? Do you favour Units over schools?

Mother: No. I think if you need schools for the deaf up to a certain age you need to give the basics in schools for the deaf. I think you need to give basics and I think you need to give this groundwork. I think if you can do that, children can then mix socially within their families in a normal atmosphere. Spend the weekends and the evenings with their parents and the rest of their family—and the holidays. I think at an early age that is what is required. I think when you get a Unit for the deaf at secondary level the advantage that large schools get over small schools is that you get the specialists. I think you need a good maths teacher, I think you need a good English teacher, who happens to be able to teach deaf children, rather than a good teacher of the deaf who can do a bit of maths. Do you see what I mean?

(These quotations are all taken from Gregory *et al.*, work in progress)

ITQ

How would you advise a hearing parent of a deaf child on placement for their deaf child?

◀ Comment
You probably have not felt happy to give advice, but would have asked questions about:

Δ   the family

Δ   the child

Δ   the available options   ◀

7.2 Deaf parents

While there have been several studies of hearing parents of deaf children, little has been reported about the feelings of deaf parents of deaf children concerning educational issues. As the main organizations representing Deaf people (the BDA, NUD) actively support the use of sign language in education, and many Deaf people are vociferous in their opposition to integration, it may be assumed that this is the stance taken by Deaf parents. It was the view put by Sandra Smith in Video One.

However, incidental evidence suggests the position is actually more complex. Certainly some deaf parents chose to use oral language with their deaf children. In an interview study of a representative group of twenty deaf parents (which excluded those with a partial hearing loss) of twenty-one young deaf children, Hartley (1988) reports that 55 per cent (11 out of 20) of the parents used mainly sign language with their children, 15 per cent (3 out of 20) used sign and speech, but 30 per cent (6 out of 20) used mainly speech. When she asked the parents whether they preferred their deaf children to play with deaf or hearing children, the parents presented a range of views:

Marcus's[9] mother:

> With deaf children most of the time, but with hearing children sometimes because hearing children can teach them language and help them with language, but deaf children can communicate better with other deaf children, so it's better for them to play with deaf children most of the time.

Zena's mother:

> I think it is difficult for a deaf child to make friends with a hearing child. (Why?) Sometimes with the deaf child they might say something and the hearing child obviously knows what's going on but the deaf child doesn't and so someone's got to explain to him and very often hearing children can't be bothered, they haven't got the time to explain everything.

[9] All names changed to respect confidentiality.

Sarah's mother:

> From my own observations I find that it does help Sarah to play with hearing children. She benefits in some ways from playing with other hearing children because she will see that the games they play have certain rules which should be obeyed by those who are playing the game and Sarah sometimes breaks the rules, not knowing why and children say 'No, you mustn't do that' ... She doesn't really fully understand it depends on the games they play but in this way I think it helps Sarah to be aware that in some games there are certain things that children can do or cannot do in order to take part in some games.
>
> (Hartley, 1988)

Overall, 71 per cent (15 out of 21) mothers thought their deaf child should play with hearing children at least some of the time, 19 per cent (4 out of 21) exclusively. Only 20 per cent (6 out of 21) advocated that their deaf child should play only with other deaf children (All findings from Hartley, 1988).

In the absence of reported material on attitudes to education, this can only be taken as suggestive information. The children were younger than school age, play preferences were not the same as school preferences and may reflect availability. However, they do reflect a flexibility in approach, an emphasis on spoken language and integration into the hearing world by some deaf parents, which is also found in deaf school-leavers, as will be shown in Section 8.

7.3 Parents of deaf children from ethnic minority groups

Earlier, it was noted that deaf children from homes where English is not the main language are seen as being 'doubly disadvantaged'. Many of these will be children from ethnic minority groups. In 1972 about 10 per cent of children in special schools for the deaf and in Partially Hearing Units were of ethnic minority origin (Department of Education and Science, 1972). The National Deaf Children's Society in 1985 estimated that percentage to be higher, though it is difficult to get precise figures. A survey of the population of the then Inner London Education Authority (ILEA) schools for the deaf and units for the partially hearing in 1983 revealed that only 52 per cent come from the British Isles, the remaining 48 per cent coming from a wide diversity of ethnic minority backgrounds. English was a second language for 20 per cent of the population (Robson, 1985).

Little is known of the parents' views, they remain largely hidden. In 1985 the NDCS published an interview by Jane Speedy, entitled 'How Do We Voice Our Problems?', with Cauline Braithwaite, a Black woman and mother of a six-year old profoundly deaf child, in which Cauline Braithwaite indicated the racism she had encountered:

JS: A lot of parents of deaf children have had similar experiences—do you think you were treated any differently by the hospital because you were black?

CB: A lot of racism is unconscious and institutionalised. I was never treated in an overtly racist way. But the doctors were really dismissive of me. They made me feel like a bad parent. I later saw that they actually thought that I was ineffectual. I saw this written down. I think that this related to the fact that I didn't force Inigo to wear his hearing aids. When Inigo first got his hearing aids, I figured it would be better if I didn't force him to wear them as I felt that he would have been more likely to resent them and refuse to wear them. After all he was only three at the time. Also he wasn't very keen on doing their tasks and they thought I should have forced him to co-operate which I didn't. They weren't interested and never seemed to listen or answer my questions. I think that white working class people get treated in a very similar way in this respect.

JS: Did you feel you got inferior treatment in any way?

CB: I certainly did. I remember once the school had written to the hospital to say that Inigo needed more powerful commercial hearing aids. Well, the consultant agreed, then they said that they weren't going to give him the more powerful hearing aids because we had lost so many and they didn't trust us. I challenged them about this. I made them go through their records and in fact he had lost only one aid and that was during the first week that he started wearing them.

JS: So maybe you were just unlucky there. What about the education system, how have you fared there?

CB: I like the school and the PHU and they do a good job—they care about hearing impaired children. However, I do feel that they could do more about putting parents in touch with each other. Having a child with a disability is a very isolating experience and this feeling of isolation is compounded in some ways by your child going to a PHU which isn't usually the local school, which means because you don't usually take the child to school or collect him or her from school you don't have the usual interaction with other parents that you would if your child went to the local school. Perhaps schools would say that it isn't their job to get involved with their families in the way that I think it could be. I also think that the school could do more to present positive images to black and hearing impaired people.

JS: What about NDCS at a national level?

CB: I don't really know about NDCS—is it for me? It seems to be all about white kids. I've noticed TALK magazine—I've been disappointed with every single copy I've seen—I haven't read it for a while though.

JS: What were you disappointed about?

CB: It's full of little white kids smiling happily in Brownie uniforms. Princess Di on the front cover—all that stuff. It could be a real pressure group thing. Why doesn't it challenge people's attitudes to disability? It's just like a coffee table magazine. It doesn't question enough, it certainly doesn't represent me as a black person.

JS: What about our other publications?

CB: Well, there are no black faces, are there? The ones for parents are all very cosy—not dishonest, but rather twee.—What about the enormous strains on family relationships? I suppose the NDCS is not for us—it's for them. I'd like to change things, I've got a lot of energy, but I'm

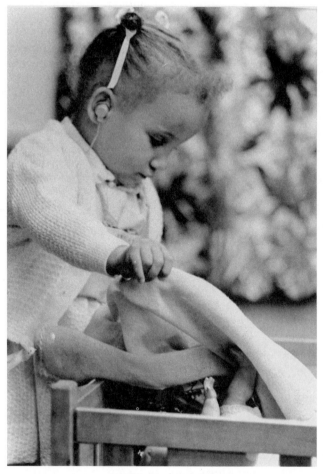

Figure 5.12 A deaf child investigates the toy box
(Source: courtesy of the Royal National Institute for the Deaf)

quite intimidated by those organisations. Black people don't get involved, not because we don't care, aren't interested or aren't dissatisfied with things.—But it is not for *us*. Black parents we talked to at school are really bewildered.

JS: And you feel it could be for you?

CB: There are very special problems for parents who have a black child with a disability in this society. How do we voice this?

(Speedy, 1985)

While the article criticizes *TALK*, its publication in that magazine indicates how seriously the NDCS took these issues in 1985. This article was one of a number of initiatives they were taking during that period as part of a process to recognize more fully the needs of families from ethnic minority groups. Even before then, *TALK* magazine had included pictures of Black and Asian children, and introduced initiatives designed to include parents of children from ethnic minority groups in their association. They are leaders in the deaf field in this respect.

The general absence of major research makes it difficult to establish how general the views of Cauline Braithwaite are. One research project, with Asian families, has been that of Rukhsana Meherali (1985), who interviewed twelve Asian families, which had eighteen deaf children aged 2½ – 3 years between them, with a range of hearing loss. The study seemed to challenge a few generally held myths—that Asian families live in large extended families and gain their support from family members; that the Asian mother is held to blame for any disability in her child. Neither of these myths was found to be the case in Meherali's study.

The concern of the families centred around language use. While none of the families used signing, most used a great deal of gesture, and while most wanted their child to learn to talk, they accepted that their child might prefer to use sign language. The following quotation is a generally representative one:

> I use gestures and speech but of course speech is very important, it's the best thing if he can manage it, so I try to make him look at my lips. If he can't learn to speak then signing is fine and I would learn it too, he's my son so it is my job to learn to communicate with him.
> (Parent of boy, 5 years of age, profoundly deaf, in Meherali, 1985)

There was some sadness that the spoken language of the child would be English, and that he or she may not learn his or her own mother tongue. Mother tongue was seen as partly embodying culture, in a parallel way to that in which sign language embodies Deaf culture and thus its loss was regretted. As we would expect, their concerns were not about Deaf culture, but their particular Asian culture. The advice given, as indicated earlier, was usually that families should use English with deaf children:

> We speak Punjabi at home but we use English with them because the school suggested it would be better for them. In a way I worry that they don't learn Punjabi because if we ever went back to Pakistan they won't be able to communicate with most people but I expect they will spend most of their lives in this country. I hope they will retain their culture and religion, because they live with us at home but of course there will be influences from the host culture. Mostly the British are good and kind, specially to the handicapped, I know my nephews in Pakistan get no schooling or training because they are deaf.
> (Parent of two boys, 8 and 2 years of age, ibid.)

Their attitudes to the help and professional advice they received was ambivalent. While most talked of the professionals as being helpful and understanding, they did not feel that explanations were very clear, and many professionals were seen as holding stereotypical and patronizing attitudes, as the following quotations indicate:

> The peripatetic teacher, Mrs. ——, she's lovely, we talk about K's progress but the nicest thing is she tells me what is happening with other hearing impaired children so I know what is possible for K. The teachers at the school are very good too, they all try to find out about our culture and religion—sometimes they have very strange ideas

about us—they think we are very backward and terribly ill-mannered but I try to put them right. I get sick of them assuming that all our women are down trodden and subservient, I'll tell you I've never met one yet, have you? They ask me why we send our children to the mosque daily to learn Urdu and Arabic and I explain that only the rural Kashmiri/Mirpuri people do that, not all Pakistanis, we are from the city and don't all behave the same way. They lump us all together don't they?

(Parent of boy, 6 years of age)

Everyone has been very helpful to us, the ones that come to the house are very supportive and kind and because they come to you you can express your needs and wants to them, even niggling little worries that you wouldn't go out to ask them. Most of the ones I've met are sensitive and interested in our culture but of course there are quite a lot of prejudiced ones—particularly when they deal with our uneducated rural people. They are all stuck on the status of women and arranged marriages without really knowing or understanding how it really is for most of our women.

(Parent of boy, 5 years of age, and girl, 3 years of age)

(Ibid.)

Perhaps it is best summed up by reporting the response of one mother to the final question in the interview, 'Is there any one message you would like to pass on to the professionals that visit you, that would help them in dealing with families from your culture?'

First of all, we are all a little bit different so don't lump us all together, be gentler with the illiterate ones, try to see that our way of life is very important to us, it is the only way we know—it may seem strange to you but we are comfortable in it—even most of the women! Secondly, help us to help our children, we want the best education for them—tell us what we can do at home to help them. Thank you for all you do and please could we have more professionals who speak our language?

(Ibid.)

8 The consumer view

The unit started with accounts by deaf people of their own education. In concluding the unit let us return to the views of deaf young people themselves—this time a group of school-leavers, who have recently been interviewed as part of a research study (Gregory *et al.*, work in progress).

This is not to assert that they have the solution. However, they were very clear about what they wanted from education, which focused, not on particular language use or school setting, but on flexibility and choice.

The interesting point revealed by the responses to the questions was the complexity of their views on language and communication, and on integration. Most accepted all language forms regardless of their own preferred language and the majority stressed the importance of the need for integration into both Deaf and hearing worlds. Interestingly, to the question on education, which asked about which setting was best, many rejected all the existing choices and proposed a modified form of integration which took more account of the needs of deaf pupils, as the following quotations show:

> There needs to be more interaction in the integrated school, everyone learning from each other not the lecturer style of teaching. There should not be one deaf child on their own but four or five in a class of hearing children. I know the feeling of being on my own—my tension and frustration. If you are with other deaf children there is a natural bond.
>
> (Deaf man, 18 years old, educated in Partially Hearing Unit and mainstream school. From notes of an interview conducted in Sign Supported English)

> They should have experience of hearing people so they learn how to communicate, but they need to sit with some deaf people so they learn about themselves.
>
> (Deaf woman, 19 years of age, educated in Partially Hearing Unit and mainstream school. From notes of an interview conducted in Sign Supported English)
>
> (Gregory *et al.*, work in progress)

Suggestions for further reading

KYLE, J. (ed.) (1987) 'Sign and school', Clevedon, Avon, in *Multilingual Matters*.
This is a collection of papers looking at theoretical and practical issues surrounding sign language used in schools.

LANE, H. (1988) *When the Mind Hears: A History of the Deaf*, Harmondsworth, Penguin.
In this book, Lane attempts to provide a history of the education of deaf children from a deaf perspective, though he himself is hearing. He takes on the persona of a Deaf man, Laurent Clerk, and writes it as a biography. It is detailed, and thoroughly researched.

STRONG, M. (ed.) (1988) *Language Learning and Deafness*, Cambridge, Cambridge University Press.
This book focuses on a wide-ranging number of issues in language learning and deafness: bilingualism in education, language and social identity, new sign creations, etc. As part of a series on applied linguistics, it is written from this perspective but is accessible to those without prior knowledge of linguistics.

WOOD, D., WOOD, H., GRIFFITHS, A. and HOWARTH, I. (1986) *Talking and Teaching with Deaf Children*, Chichester, Wiley.
While the deaf children studied in this book are being educated in the oralist tradition, and this may be seen as a limitation, the presentation goes beyond discussions of mode of communication and examines teacher style, dialogue and communication, as well as considering attainments in mathematics and English.

References

ARNOLD, P. (1988) 'The integration of deaf children into ordinary schools', *Journal of the Australian Teachers of the Deaf*, no. 29.

ARNOLD, T. (1879) *Aures Surdis: The Education of the Deaf and Dumb*, London, Elliot Stock.

BENDER, R. (1970) *The Conquest of Deafness*, Cleveland, OH, Case Western Reserve.

BOOTH, T. (1988) 'Challenging conceptions of integration', in Gregory, S. and Hartley, G.M. (eds) (1990) *Constructing Deafness*, London, Pinter Publishers. (D251 Reader Two, Article 5.10)

BRIGGS, L. (1990) 'A polytechnic with a difference', in Taylor, G. and Bishop, J. (eds) (1990) *Being Deaf: The Experience of Deafness*, London, Pinter Publishers. (D251 Reader One, Article 12)

BRITISH ASSOCIATION OF TEACHERS OF THE DEAF (1985) 'Audiological descriptors', in Gregory, S. and Hartley, G.M. (eds) (1990) *Constructing Deafness*, London, Pinter Publishers. (D251 Reader Two, Article 5.1)

BULLOCK REPORT (1975) *A Language for Life*, London, HMSO.

CONRAD, R. (1979a) *The Deaf School Child: Language and Cognitive Function*, London, Harper and Row.

CONRAD, R. (1979b) 'The deaf school child', in Gregory, S. and Hartley, G.M. (eds) (1990) *Constructing Deafness*, London, Pinter Publishers. (D251 Reader Two, Article 5.4)

CORSON, H.M. (1973) *Comparing Deaf Children of Oral Parents and Deaf Parents Using Manual Communication with Deaf Children of Hearing Parents on Academic, Social and Communication Functioning*, unpublished doctoral dissertation, Ohio, University of Cincinnati.

CRADDOCK, E. (1990) 'Life at secondary school', in Taylor, G. and Bishop, J. (eds) (1990) *Being Deaf: The Experience of Deafness*, London, Pinter Publishers. (D251 Reader One, Article 11)

CUMMINS, J. and SWAIN, M. (1986) *Bilingualism in Education*, Longman.

DEPARTMENT OF EDUCATION AND SCIENCE (1972) *Statistics of Education*, London, HMSO.

ELSEY, S. (1990) 'Training to teach', in Taylor, G. and Bishop, J. (eds) (1990) *Being Deaf: The Experience of Deafness*, London, Pinter Publishers. (D251 Reader One, Article 14)

EVANS, L. (1982) 'Total communication', in Gregory, S. and Hartley, G.M. (eds) (1990) *Constructing Deafness*, London, Pinter Publishers. (D251 Reader Two, Article 5.6)

FLETCHER, L. (1987) 'Deafness: the treatment', in Taylor, G. and Bishop, J. (eds) (1990) *Being Deaf: The Experience of Deafness*, London, Pinter Publishers. (D251 Reader One, Article 7)

GOODWILL, J. (1990) 'Janet's diary', in Taylor, G. and Bishop, J. (eds) (1990) *Being Deaf: The Experience of Deafness*, London, Pinter Publishers. (D251 Reader One, Article 1)

GRANT, B. (1990) *The Deaf Advance: A History of the British Deaf Association 1890–1990*, East Lothian, Pentland Press.

GREGORY, S. (1987) 'Review of Lynas, W., "Integrating the handicapped into ordinary schools"', *British Deaf News*, vol. 18, no. 2.

GREGORY, S. and BISHOP, J. (1989) 'The mainstreaming of primary age deaf children', in Gregory, S. and Hartley, G.M. (eds) (1990) *Constructing Deafness*, London, Pinter Publishers. (D251 Reader Two, Article 5.11)

GREGORY, S., BISHOP, J. and SHELDON, L. (work in progress) *Deaf Young People Growing Up* (working title).

GREGORY, S. and HARTLEY, G. (eds) (1990) *Constructing Deafness*, London, Pinter Publishers. (D251 Reader Two)

GREGORY, S. and MEHERALI, R. (1986) 'A need for action', *TALK*, no. 122.

HARRISON, D. (1986) 'The education of hearing impaired children in local schools—a survey', *Journal of the British Association of Teachers of the Deaf*, vol. 10, no. 4.

HARTLEY, G. (1988) *Aspects of the Home Care of Young Deaf Children of Deaf Parents*, PhD thesis, University of Nottingham.

HODGSON, K. (1954) *The Deaf and Their Problems*, New York, Philosophical Library.

HOLEHOUSE, P. (1990) 'From college to work in the lace industry', in Taylor, G. and Bishop, J. (eds) (1990) *Being Deaf: The Experience of Deafness*, London, Pinter Publishers. (D251 Reader One, Article 16)

JENSEMA, C.J. and TRYBUS, R.J. (1978) *Communication Patterns and Educational Achievement*, Washington, DC, Office of Demographic Studies, Gallaudet College.

JOHNSON, R.E., LIDDELL, S.K. and ERTING, C.J. (1989) *Unlocking the Curriculum: Principles for Achieving Access in Deaf Education*, Gallaudet Research Institute Working Paper, 89–3, Washington, DC, Gallaudet University.

JONES, J. (1985) 'Leadership in the deaf community', *Journal of the National Council of Social Workers with Deaf People*, vol. 1, no. 2.

KITTEL, R. (1989) 'Total commitment to total communication', in Taylor, G. and Bishop, J. (eds) (1990) *Being Deaf: The Experience of Deafness*, London, Pinter Publishers. (D251 Reader One, Article 5)

KYLE, J. (1986) 'Deaf people and minority groups in the UK', in Gregory, S. and Hartley, G.M. (eds) (1990) *Constructing Deafness*, London, Pinter Publishers. (D251 Reader Two, Article 7.7)

KYLE, J. and WOLL, B. (1985) *Sign Language: The Study of Deaf People and Their Language*, Cambridge, Cambridge University Press. (D251 Set Book)

LADD, P. (1981) 'Making plans for Nigel: the erosion of indentity by mainstreaming', in Taylor, G. and Bishop, J. (eds) (1990) *Being Deaf: The Experience of Deafness*, London, Pinter Publishers. (D251 Reader One, Article 10)

LANE, H. (1984) 'Why the Deaf Are angry', in Gregory, S. and Hartley, G.M. (eds) (1990) *Constructing Deafness*, London, Pinter Publishers. (D251 Reader Two, Article 5.3)

LANE, H. (1988) *When the Mind Hears*, London, Penguin.

LEWIS REPORT, DEPARTMENT OF EDUCATION AND SCIENCE (1968) *The Education of Deaf Children: The Possible Place of Finger Spelling and Signing* (The Lewis Report), London, HMSO.

LINGUISTIC MINORITIES PROJECT (1985) *The Other Languages of England*, London, Routledge.

LLWELLYN-JONES, M. (1987) 'Bilingualism and the education of deaf children', in Gregory, S. and Hartley, G.M. (eds) (1990) *Constructing Deafness*, London, Pinter Publishers. (D251 Reader Two, Article 5.7)

LYNAS, W. (1984) 'The education of hearing impaired pupils in ordinary schools: integration or pseudo assimilation?', *Journal of the British Association of Teachers of the Deaf* , vol. 8, no. 5.

LYNAS, W. (1986a) *Integrating the Handicapped into Ordinary Schools: A Study of Hearing Impaired Pupils*, London, Croom Helm.

LYNAS, W. (1986b) 'Integrating the handicapped into ordinary schools', in Gregory, S. and Hartley, G.M. (eds) (1990) *Constructing Deafness*, London, Pinter Publishers. (D251 Reader Two, Article 5.9)

LYNAS, W., HUNTINGTON, A. and TUCKER, I. (1988) 'A critical examination of different approaches to communication in the education of deaf children', in Gregory, S. and Hartley, G.M. (eds) (1990) *Constructing Deafness*, London, Pinter Publishers. (D251 Reader Two, Article 5.5)

MACDONALD, H. (1989) 'The chance to speak for ourselves', in Taylor, G. and Bishop, J. (eds) (1990) *Being Deaf: The Experience of Deafness*, London, Pinter Publishers. (D251 Reader One, Article 6)

MARKIDES, A. (1983a) *The Speech of Hearing Impaired Children,* Manchester, Manchester University Press.

MARKIDES, A. (1983b) 'The teaching of speech: historical developments', in Gregory, S. and Hartley, G.M. (eds) (1990) *Constructing Deafness*, London, Pinter Publishers. (D251 Reader Two, Article 5.2)

MASON, C. (1990) 'School experiences', in Taylor, G. and Bishop, J. (eds) (1990) *Being Deaf: The Experience of Deafness*, London, Pinter Publishers. (D251 Reader One, Article 9)

MCLOUGHLIN, M.G. (1987) *A History of Education of the Deaf in England and Wales*, Liverpool, G.M. McLoughlin.

MEADOW, K. (1967) *The Effect of Early Manual Communication and Family Climate on the Deaf Child's Development,* unpublished doctoral dissertation, Berkeley, CA, University of California.

MEHERALI, R. (1985) *The Deaf Asian Child and His Family*, dissertation submitted in partial requirement for an MA, University of Nottingham, Child Development Research Unit.

MINISTRY OF EDUCATION CIRCULAR, 10/62 (1962) London, HMSO.

MONERY, C. and JANES, L. (1990) 'School—the early years', in Taylor, G. and Bishop, J. (eds) (1990) *Being Deaf: The Experience of Deafness*, London, Pinter Publishers. (D251 Reader One, Article 8)

MOORES, D. (1978) *Educating the Deaf: Psychology, Principles and Practices*, London, Houghton Mifflin Co.

NATIONAL UNION OF THE DEAF (not dated, circa 1982) *Charter of Rights of the Deaf, Part One, The Rights of the Deaf Child*, Guildford, National Union of the Deaf.

PADDEN, C. and HUMPHRIES, T. (1988) *Deaf in America*, London, Harvard University Press.

PAUL, P.V. (1988) 'American Sign Language and English: A Bilingual Minority Language Immersion, Programme CAID—News 'N' Notes', Washington, DC, Conference of American Institutions of the Deaf, quoted in Johnson *et al.* (1989).

QUIGLEY, S. and FRINSINA, D. (1961) *Institutionalization of Psychoeducational Developments of Deaf Children*, CEC Research Monograph, Urbana, Illinois.

QUIGLEY, S. and KRETSCHMER, R.E. (1982) *The Education of Deaf Children*, London, Edward Arnold.

REID, C. (1990) 'Education for life?', in Taylor, G. and Bishop, J. (eds) (1990) *Being Deaf: The Experience of Deafness*, London, Pinter Publishers. (D251 Reader One, Article 13)

ROBINSON, K. (1987) 'A toy merry-go-round', in Taylor, G. and Bishop, J. (eds) (1990) *Being Deaf: The Experience of Deafness*, London, Pinter Publishers. (D251 Reader One, Article 4)

ROBSON, P. (1985) 'The challenge facing all those in special education', *TALK*, no. 118.

SHAW, R. (1990) 'A career in design', in Taylor, G. and Bishop, J. (eds) (1990) *Being Deaf: The Experience of Deafness*, London, Pinter Publishers. (D251 Reader One, Article 15)

SILO, J. (1990) 'A deaf teacher: a personal odyssey', in Taylor, G. and Bishop, J. (eds) (1990) *Being Deaf: The Experience of Deafness*, London, Pinter Publishers. (D251 Reader One, Article 19)

SILO, J. (work in progress) *The Role of Deaf Teachers in the Education of Deaf Children*, MPhil in preparation, Milton Keynes, The Open University.

SNOWDON WORKING PARTY (1976) *Integrating the Disabled*, London, The National Fund for Research into Crippling Diseases.

SPEEDY, J. (1985) 'How do we voice our problems?', *TALK*, no. 118.

SPEEDY, J. (1987) 'Breaking down barriers', *TALK*, no. 125.

STUCKLESS, R. and BIRCH, J.J. (1966) 'The influence of early manual communication on the linguistic development of deaf children', *American Annals of the Deaf*, vol. 111.

SUPPES, P. (1974) 'Cognition in handicapped children', *Review of Educational Research*, vol. 44.

SWANN REPORT (1985) *Education for All*, Committee of Enquiry into Education of Children from Ethnic Minority Groups, London, HMSO.

TAYLOR, G. and BISHOP, J. (eds) (1990) *Being Deaf: The Experience of Deafness*, London, Pinter Publishers. (D251 Reader One)

TUCKER, I. and NOLAN, M. (1984) *Educational Audiology*, London, Croom Helm.

VERNON, M. and KOH, S. (1970) 'Early manual communication and deaf children's achievement', *American Annals of the Deaf,* vol. 115.

WARNOCK REPORT (1978) *A Report of the Committee of Enquiry into the Education of Handicapped Children and Young People,* London, HMSO.

WOOD, D., WOOD, H., GRIFFITHS, A. and HOWARTH, I. (1986a) *Talking and Teaching with Deaf Children,* Chichester, Wiley.

WOOD, D., WOOD, H., GRIFFITHS, A. and HOWARTH, I. (1986b) 'Teaching and talking with deaf children', in Gregory, S. and Hartley, G.M. (eds) (1990) *Constructing Deafness,* London, Pinter Publishers. (D251 Reader Two, Article 5.8)

WOOD, D., WOOD, H. and KINGSMALL, M. (submitted for publication) *Signed English in the Classroom,* a monograph.

Acknowledgements

Grateful acknowledgement is made to the following sources for permission to reproduce material in this unit:

Text

Speedy, J. 'How do we voice our problems?', *Talk Magazine,* National Deaf Children's Society, no. 118, winter 1985, © NDCS.

Tables

Table 5.1 Wood, D., Wood, H., Griffith, A. and Howarth, I. *Talking and Teaching with Deaf Children,* p. 151, table 9.1, © 1986 John Wiley and Sons Ltd, reprinted by permission of John Wiley and Sons Ltd; *Table 5.2* Lynas, W. *Integrating the Handicapped into Ordinary Schools,* Croom Helm, 1986.

Figures

Figures 5.1, 5.2, 5.3, 5.11, 5.12 The Royal National Institute for the Deaf; *Figures 5.4, 5.5, 5.6, 5.7, 5.9, 5.10* Terry Boyle, photographer, and Miranda Pickersgill; *Figure 5.8* The Royal School for the Deaf, Derby.

Grateful acknowledgement is made to Trevor Landell for permission to use his painting on the covers and title pages throughout the units of this course.

Unit 6 The Manufacture of Disadvantage

prepared for the course team by George Taylor and Carlo Laurenzi

Contents

Associated study materials

Video Three, *Deaf People and Mental Health*

Reader One, Article 25, 'Provision for Deaf Patients in Rampton Special Hospital', Janet Goodwill and Rae Than.

Reader Two, Article 3.1, 'Cognition and Language', Stephen Quigley and Peter Paul.

Reader Two, Article 3.2, 'Looking for Meaning in Sign Language Sentences', Jim Kyle.

Reader Two, Article 3.3, 'Surdophrenia', Terje Basilier.

Reader Two, Article 3.4, 'Is there a "Psychology of the Deaf"?', Harlan Lane.

D251 Issues in Deafness

Unit 1   *Perspectives on Deafness: An Introduction*

Block 1   Being Deaf
Unit 2   *The Deaf Community*
Unit 3   *British Sign Language, Communication and Deafness*
Unit 4   *The Other Deaf Community?*

Block 2   Deaf People in Hearing Worlds
Unit 5   *Education and Deaf People: Learning to Communicate or Communicating to Learn?*
Unit 6   *The Manufacture of Disadvantage*
Unit 7   *Whose Welfare?*

Block 3   Constructing Deafness
Unit 8   *The Social Construction of Deafness*
Unit 9   *Deaf People as a Minority Group: The Political Process*
Unit 10 *Deaf Futures*

Readers

Reader One: Taylor, G. and Bishop, J. (eds) (1990) *Being Deaf: The Experience of Deafness*, London, Pinter Publishers.

Reader Two: Gregory, S. and Hartley, G.M. (eds) (1990) *Constructing Deafness*, London, Pinter Publishers.

Set Books

Kyle, J. and Woll, B. (1985) *Sign Language: The Study of Deaf People and Their Language*, Cambridge, Cambridge University Press.

Miles, D. (1988) *British Sign Language: A Beginner's Guide*, London, BBC Books (BBC Enterprises). With a chapter by Paddy Ladd.

Videotapes

Video One   *Sandra's Story: The History of a Deaf Family*
Video Two   *Sign Language*
Video Three *Deaf People and Mental Health*
Video Four   *Signs of Change: Politics and the Deaf Community*

Aims

The aims of this unit are:

1 To describe and discuss the specialist mental health services available to Deaf people in Britain.

2 To explore the suitability of the general mental health system for Deaf users.

3 To examine the discourses of medicine, psychology and psychiatry for their relevance to Deaf people.

4 To explore the notion that there is a 'psychology of deafness', and to consider the implications of this.

5 To consider the potential and actual changes in mental health services for deaf people brought about by changes in social policy, developments in professional practice, and the involvement of more deaf people as workers within the system.

Study guide

The issues raised in this unit are intricate and should be approached with some care, not only because of their technical complexity, but also because many of the ideas and beliefs involved in the debates transcend professional boundaries to become embedded in the currency of everyday life and 'common-sense' or 'logical' notions.

We suggest that a good way to study this unit would be to read it through fairly quickly to begin with, ignoring the activities, ITQs and references to the Reader articles and the video. This will give you an idea of the breadth of the subject being covered and alert you to some of the issues involved. You should then be able to plan your detailed study of the unit more effectively by identifying those areas you think may take more of your time.

Introduction

It is understandable that we should be attracted by the belief that mental disorders are conditions arising from social existence rather than biological processes, and the correlative hope that the miseries engendered by unemployment, sexual incompatibility, infertility, bad housing, poverty, urban decay, violence, troublesome children and so forth might be solved or ameliorated by psychiatric knowledge and expertise. But rather than extending the remit of psychiatry to the manifold problems of social and personal life, should we not ask of psychiatry that it takes as its rationale the problem of cure rather than the project of normalization?

(Miller and Rose, 1986)

This unit is about the way the mental health system in the UK responds to the needs of Deaf people, and, more specifically, the specialist facilities that exist for Deaf people. It is pertinent to ask why services have developed in their current form and how these services are prioritized. The answers to these questions lie not with Deaf users of the mental health system, but with the structure and processes of the system itself, and with the behaviour of professionals, not with the behaviour of Deaf people.

This unit, therefore, is *not* an investigation of Deaf people within the mental health system. Rather, it is an examination of the discourses on deafness that promote particular professional practices, and how these discourses are embedded within the structure and operation of the mental health system as it is available to Deaf people.

Deaf people are a minority of the general population of the UK and, not surprisingly, psychiatric services specifically for Deaf people are few and far between. If the problem were simply one of numbers then it would be more easily addressed. Most people in society do not have need of the services of psychiatrists, and this is also the case for Deaf people. Therefore, the demand for psychiatric help for Deaf people must be small and this should be reflected by the general availability of services.

There are two major problems with this line of thought, however. First, demography: Deaf people live in all parts of the UK, so services may be required in Aberdeen one day, Aberystwyth the next, and Aberford the following. This therefore gives rise to an issue about where services should be located. The second problem is developing practice: because mental health personnel see so few 'mentally ill' deaf people, the accumulation of case material is a long and painstaking process.

There may be a danger that generalizations are made on the basis of just a few case histories, otherwise the 'knowledge' base of psychiatric services for Deaf people may appear to be at a standstill. The danger of generalizing about Deaf people is that they do not conform to any particular type. As you learnt in Unit 4, like hearing people their beliefs and behaviours are also influenced by whether they are Black or white, blind or sighted, gay or straight, older or younger, male or female and so on.

Some people believe that there is a distinct Deaf personality type and that its features are identifiable and available for scientific enquiry. In Sections 2 and 3 of this unit we will be considering the 'medical model' as a major influence on the nature of psychiatric services for Deaf people. A 'medical model' construction of deafness is that deafness is a deficiency, a disease, that requires treatment. Surgery is one of the responses to the physical aspects of deafness. There is also a view that deafness has psychological consequences, that it leads to the development of a particular personality structure (surdophrenia), which locates it as a legitimate area for psychiatric management. Together with general developments in the field of psychology in the areas of social categorization, individualization and notions of 'normal' behaviour, Deaf people have increasingly become the subjects of psychological study. We explore some of the findings of this particular type of research and the effect it has upon specialist psychiatric services.

Following this, we will look in some detail at the issues raised as Deaf people come face-to-face with the process of the mental health system, from the initial referral, through assessment and diagnosis, to treatment. How does the mental health system respond to Deaf people? Do they get a fair deal? And what safeguards are there that the assistance they receive will be appropriate to their needs? As Rack writes:

> Irrespective of cultural differences, what the practitioner perceives is not a *person* but a *problem*. 'It' is a housing application, a broken arm, an outburst of seemingly crazy behaviour, or a petty larceny. The bearer of the problem is a faceless, indistinct figure. As the conversation or interview gets under way, a picture begins to emerge. The overall shape becomes visible first, followed by increasing detail. The client tries to 'develop' first those details which seem to him (*sic*) most relevant to the immediate problem. The practitioner fills in some of the gaps with direct questions. What started as a two-dimensional outline figure becomes recognizable as a unique individual. The practitioner no longer sees a problem, but *a person with a problem.*
>
> (Rack, 1982)

The personnel in the mental health system are mostly hearing people, so for a Deaf person this relationship immediately raises issues of language, culture and power. It is an area charged with the hazard of misunderstandings, which for the Deaf person could result in a curtailment of his or her liberty. For example, a Deaf woman who told her doctor about the electricity in her head was thought to be having a psychotic episode, whereas she was actually referring to the brain activity associated with epilepsy, and her fears that her children may 'inherit' the condition.

Even with well developed communication skills, hearing professionals are mostly charting unknown territory in such situations. A major factor in the relationship between the hearing professional and the Deaf person is that of difference. What does difference mean in this context? Are Deaf people different because they are a minority in a hearing society? And is their difference celebrated or seen as a problem? When it comes to trying to understand the behaviour of Deaf people with whom they come into contact, do professionals in the mental health system compare the behaviour of Deaf people with what is considered 'normal' or acceptable within the hearing majority? Or do they have their own ideas about what 'normality' is within the Deaf community?

In Section 12 we will be looking at the contribution made by those professionals who are themselves deaf. What is the extent of their involvement? Are they being employed in key positions? And, does having a 'Deaf perspective' mean that they are able to work in a way that hearing people are not? Daniel Langholtz is a Deaf person and a therapist. He offers his view of the value of Deaf professionals in the system which is a distillation of his own client's comments: '*Langholtz's client:* I don't have to take up too much time explaining what it is like to be deaf; you already know all that and you respect the cultural aspects of my deafness' (Elliott *et al.*, 1987). Whether or not the involvement of deaf professionals in the mental health system is without problems will be explored in more depth.

At the time of writing, local authorities are beginning to formulate their plans for 'community care' packages in response to developing legislation. But is community care a good idea? Or is it, in reality, benign neglect? A great deal of the rhetoric of community alternatives is based on a critique of the asylums. However, it is important to note that the asylums originated as a response to the unsatisfactory nature of community solutions. 'Community' itself is an unsatisfactory term of reference with an almost infinite range of meanings and interpretations. As society develops and changes so 'community' is also subject to competing explanations. As Scull comments, the concept of 'community' conjures up: '... a mythical "Golden Age", an innocent robust society uncorrupted by bureaucracy, where neighbour helps neighbour, and families willingly minister to the needs of their own troublesome members, whilst a benevolent and indulgent squirearchy looks on always ready to lend a helping hand' (Scull, 1977).

Unit 4 raised some of the issues involved in the 'romantic' view of community, as criticized by Scull. In Section 13 of this unit we will be examining the consequences of the developing notions of community care for deaf people in the mental health system.

Finally, the terms 'mental illness' and 'mentally ill' will be used throughout this unit, but the definitions of such terms are not without problems and a general definition of mental illness is difficult to establish. Mental illness is not a thing you can see or touch, it must first of all be described in order to appear 'real'. This process, and the different ways of describing mental illness, are the focus of current academic and professional debate, as is the way that much of the language used in psychiatry and psychology is also used in wider society, and the extent to which personal difficulties are thus increasingly viewed as legitimately available for psychiatric intervention.

◀ Activity 1

There are two questions we would like you to bear in mind as you work through the unit:

(a) What are the major factors that influence the way in which Deaf people are perceived by psychiatric personnel?

(b) Should the personal and social problems of Deaf people be the concern of psychiatric personnel?

Make some notes on your response to these questions now. These are themes that run throughout the unit and we shall return to them at the end. ◀

1 Psychiatric services for Deaf people

Prelingually profoundly deaf people are no more likely to suffer from frank mental illness than the hearing population. However, they tend to spend longer periods in mental hospitals than hearing people because their communication problems interfere with both diagnosis and treatment.

(Denmark, in British Deaf Association, 1984)

At the time of writing there are two psychiatric units for Deaf people in Britain. Until 1968 there was none.

The Department of Psychiatry for the Deaf in Whittingham Hospital, near Preston, was established in 1968 under the aegis of Dr John Denmark (although an out-patient facility had existed in Manchester since 1964). It was originally designed to meet the needs of mentally ill prelingually Deaf adults. It now offers a service to a wider patient group to include all ages, all communication needs, and a greater spread of presenting problems. The Unit provides in-patient care for twenty-four people and care for about fifteen people in the local community. Organization is on multi-disciplinary/consensus management lines, with patient participation through weekly staff/patient meetings. The expressed aim of the Unit is to produce a 'therapeutic community' milieu through increasing use of rehabilitative programmes.

Springfield Hospital, in south London, started with a small group of Deaf patients 2 days a week in 1971; the psychiatric unit was then set up in 1974. This special unit has facilities for twenty in-patients and eighteen day-patients at any one time: numbers of day-patients total about 250 per annum. Much emphasis is placed upon developing community care facilities: to date there are two hostels, three houses for independent living, a day centre, and an arrangement with the local authority to place ex-patients in council flats. There is also a Community Support Team consisting of four nurses, a social worker and an occupational therapist.

The case for a specialist psychiatric service for Deaf people was first argued in Britain by John Denmark (Denmark, 1966), following a survey of profoundly Deaf patients in two mental hospitals in the North of England.

> From our sample it would appear that there are a far greater number of born deaf persons in mental hospitals than would be expected from the incidence of deafness in the general population. In our series the average length of stay was twenty years four months. This is probably far greater than the average length of stay of the overall population and would account for the high incidence of deaf persons in mental hospitals. The increased length of stay is, in all probability, due to the fact that the diagnostic difficulty results in inadequate treatment. The frequent history of disturbed behaviour in deaf patients may also delay discharge due to apprehension about possible recurrence.
>
> (Denmark, 1966)

Although Denmark's study was done some time ago, the situation has changed little since then, according to Ludo Timmermans of Belgium. In a paper delivered to the First European Congress on Mental Health and Deafness in 1988, Timmermans reported the results of his 1985 study which demonstrate that deaf patients in psychiatric hospitals are resident for an average of 21 years, compared with 148 days for hearing patients.

In his study, Denmark identified diagnosis as the major problem, and we shall look at this later in Section 10. The other difficulty foreseen by Denmark was that of the small numbers of Deaf people who require such a service and of their scattered locations. Local, or even regional, services would be difficult to justify in terms of capital outlay and maintenance costs, so Denmark proposed: '... the establishment of a unit for the assessment and rehabilitation of long-term patients' (Denmark, 1966). When we asked about the current populations of Deaf patients in both Whittingham and Springfield, we were told that of the small population of Deaf people residing as in-patients, by far the most common condition diagnosed is described by the consultant psychiatrists as 'behavioural disorder'. Essentially, this means that their behaviour is antisocial, possibly self-destructive, aggressive and of sufficient degree to warrant their removal from the community. Yet behavioural disorders amongst the hearing population can be and are treated successfully through a variety of rehabilitation programmes in the community, so why are these people in a psychiatric hospital?

ITQ

Can you think of an explanation that might account for the extended stay of Deaf patients in psychiatric hospitals? And might this explanation also account for the disproportionate numbers of Deaf people with 'behavioural disorders' in the specialist psychiatric hospitals? Make a few notes on your responses to these questions before reading further. (At this stage we do not expect you to be able to answer these questions fully, but we raise them now as it is important that you have them in mind as you work through the unit.)

One possible explanation might be that there are few opportunities in the training of psychiatrists that enable them to work with Deaf people, and the body of knowledge is thus very slim. Funding authorities would be unlikely to support relatively expensive (in their view) facilities for a very

Figure 6.1 Richardson House rehabilitation centre, Blackburn
(Source: courtesy of the Royal National Institute for the Deaf)

8

Figure 6.2 Court Grange social and vocational training centre, Devon
(Source: courtesy of the Royal National Institute for the Deaf)

small group of mentally ill patients, and so the two specialist units may be forced into widening their sphere of interests in order to be 'cost-effective'.

Another possible explanation is a lack of resources. Once the assessment has been completed by the specialist psychiatric unit, and it is decided that the Deaf person is not mentally ill but would benefit from a rehabilitation programme, where might he or she go? At present, there are three main options: Court Grange in Devon, Richardson House in Blackburn and the Hayfields Rehabilitation Unit in Scotland.

Court Grange is owned and run by the Royal National Institute for the Deaf (RNID). It provides a social training function for 'emotionally unstable and/ or psychologically disturbed' Deaf men between the ages of 16 and 22. Many of the residents of Court Grange have severe behavioural problems and convictions for criminal offences. The aim is to restore residents to society equipped to live as independently as possible.

Richardson House is also owned and run by the RNID. It can accommodate twenty-six residents aged from 16 to 40, and the aim is to help individuals to achieve their 'maximum potential', and to prepare residents to live in the community. Applicants must have a history of mental illness or behavioural problems, and be capable of benefiting from the rehabilitation programme.

The Hayfields Rehabilitation Unit is independently owned and managed. It offers both day and residential provision to deaf people between 16 and 45 years. The aim of the Unit is to 'provide education and training in social and independence skills', with the long-term objective of a return to the community. Most of the deaf people in the Unit are having to learn these skills for the first time.

The lack of resources explanation would appear to have some substance. For example, what happens to Deaf people over the age of 45 who need rehabilitation? With only three rehabilitation units, one of which, Court Grange, aims at only one section of the community, the problem of geographical spread has not been alleviated. Unless patients live near one of the two psychiatric hospitals or near one of the rehabilitation units, they will inevitably be uprooted from their home area in order to receive the help they need.

It is also significant that, whilst in-patient care in hospital is a state provision, there are no state-funded rehabilitation schemes other than those attached to the hospitals, despite the obvious need for a community-based service. This has the effect of ensuring that rehabilitation work with Deaf people stays firmly within the remit of the hospital. A recommendation by a psychiatrist for a programme of rehabilitation for a Deaf person, carries little weight if the money cannot be found (usually from the Deaf person's local authority) to pay for a place in a specialist rehabilitation unit. Payment for this type of provision would usually come from the local authority's 'adult care' budget. However, if the policy of the local authority is not to finance 'external' residential provision for 'adult care' (quite a common policy with escalating local authority costs for child care), then perhaps the hospitals are forced into developing their own facilities.

As Busfield comments:

> The impact of the social and economic organization of medical work can be seen most clearly in situations where the relationship between practitioners and patients is mediated by some third party involved in the financing of medicine, whether it be the state or some providential or profit making insurance company, for the financial policies of this third party will reduce clinical autonomy.
>
> (Busfield, 1986)

2 The influence of the medical model

We will be looking more closely at the issues surrounding 'community care' for psychiatric patients in Section 13. For now we will turn our attention to the medical profession itself, to see how the medical view of deafness influences specialist psychiatric services for Deaf people.

Doctors, according to Illich, are empowered to comment upon all aspects of life, so much so that all areas of human reproduction, development and ageing have been medicalized to such an extent that doctors transcend the limits of 'legitimate' medical intervention and act as agents of social regulation, offering a diagnosis to anything that is out of step with the rest of society:

> Diagnosis transfers the reason for the individual's breakdown from the engineered environment to the organism which does not fit. Disease thus takes on its own substance within the body of the person. The doctor shapes and defines it for the patient. The classification of

10

disease (nosology) that society adopts mirrors its institutional structure, and the sickness which is engendered by this structure is interpreted for the patient in the language the institutions have generated.

(Illich, 1975)

However, doctors have only relatively recently been elevated to this 'privileged' position. Until about the eighteenth century, the treatment and cure of physical illness was handled in a very different way (by herbalists and local healers, for instance), and mental illness was seen as the responsibility of the clergy. The growth of science in recent centuries has provided the reference point for a whole range of developing professions, and doctors see themselves as practising a science rather than an art. The intensive urbanization of Britain during, and since, the Industrial Revolution has provided the raw material for doctors to experiment and establish their knowledge base and methodology.

The power of the medical profession was clearly demonstrated at the point when the National Health Service (NHS) was established in 1948. The whole exercise almost failed because consultants and general practitioners (GPs) refused to become employees of the NHS. The system continues to creak along unsatisfactorily, with the bulk of the work being done by poorly paid NHS employees (nurses, junior hospital doctors and ancillary staff, for example), whilst the major decisions are made by well-paid consultants who are not employed by the NHS and whose decisions or conduct cannot be challenged other than through recourse to law.

A major difficulty with the medical model is that practitioners expect it to accommodate every situation within the current knowledge base. A further difficulty is that the 'problem' is identified as being *within* the individual, and the treatment is administered accordingly regardless of the source of the problem. An example of this is when women are prescribed tranquillizers for 'bad nerves', when 'bad nerves' are in fact often related to such external issues as isolation, inadequate housing, financial problems, or domestic violence. Nevertheless, the person seeking help is frequently diagnosed as 'sick' and therefore given treatment.

In the way that diagnosis is a reflection of societal values, so treatment is a reflection of whatever scientific knowledge is available. As the knowledge base grows and shifts, new treatments become available to a range of diagnoses that constantly alter according to the extent of the diagnosing doctor's knowledge base and to discourses that influence the regulation of society at any given time. So, for instance, homosexuality, which until relatively recently was a diagnosable illness, has stopped being an illness due to society's shifting value system and not as a result of any medical breakthrough. 'Bleeding' through the application of leeches, on the other hand, was discontinued because it was discovered that 'bleeding' a sick person was more harmful than curative.

When confronted with deafness, the medical model encounters severe difficulties. Early profound deafness is incurable, intractable and permanent, and is therefore a very unattractive proposition for medical practitioners.

The curative power of medical treatment is an important issue here, because the medical profession is perceived as being responsible for the discovery and provision of cures. The romantic image of the doctor is that 'he' (in the romantic image the doctor is always male) is either studiously following clues like a detective to discover the cause of his patient's pain, or he is slaving away into the night over a Bunsen burner trying to find a cure to an incurable illness. The notion of diagnosis and cure underpins the way in which doctors work and gives them the licence mentioned earlier to comment upon all spheres of human activity. It is the concentration upon (if not the obsession with) sickness that fosters the notion that there is no such thing as a truly healthy person because we all have the potential to become sick. For this reason doctors find it very easy to diagnose someone as being sick, but extremely difficult to pronounce that they are well.

Doctors are not alone in their less than enthusiastic response to profoundly Deaf people. Society generally has an ill-informed and prejudicial view of Deaf people. Categorized as 'outsiders' like people with disabilities, ethnic minorities and gay groups, Deaf people bear a 'social stigma'. But whereas someone in a wheelchair, or with a limb missing, is clearly identified as being 'disabled', deafness is hidden, and hearing people can easily be surprised by Deaf people. This is particularly relevant because deafness is of relatively low-prevalence and many hearing people will have no experience of meeting with Deaf people. The open display of a disability is important to able-bodied people because it allows them the choice of encountering (without being surprised) or avoiding the person with a disability. Hearing people are so severely handicapped in communicating with a profoundly Deaf person that most people will avoid the encounter and the possibility of embarrassment. Without the direct experience of meeting and knowing deaf people, their understanding of deafness is informed by general societal attitudes.

From early history deaf people have been subject to the erroneous assumptions of hearing people based upon ignorance and fear:

> In its earliest and most extreme form, the assumption was based upon the following argument: Thinking cannot develop without language, language, in turn, cannot develop without speech. (Language and speech were often seen as synonymous.) Speech cannot develop without hearing. Therefore those who cannot hear cannot think.
>
> (Higgins, 1980)

3 A Deaf personality?

One view of Deaf people is that they are rigid thinkers, aggressive, of low intelligence and incapable of complex thought and that these traits are somehow directly the result of early profound deafness. Furthermore, these notions are not confined to those who know little or nothing about Deaf people. We have heard these statements uttered by children of Deaf people as well as by teachers and social workers, and other professionals who specialize in working with Deaf people.

A concept which is currently popular in the study of the behaviour of Deaf people is that of 'surdophrenia', which we will ask you to read about in the Reader article by Terje Basilier in a moment. Surdophrenia, as coined by Basilier, is the 'psychic consequences of congenital or early acquired deafness'. This notion of the 'Deaf mind', or 'Deaf personality', is one that has been widely accepted by professionals in the field of deafness. Basilier concludes by stating that: 'Our experiences are that congenital or early acquired deafness may give a certain personality structure—a surdophrenia—and that deaf persons with nervous reactions are in need of specialized psychiatric service' (Basilier, 1964b). But is the concept of surdophrenia helpful to Deaf people? And how do the assumptions and theories that underpin surdophrenia relate to other mechanisms for social regulation when applied not only to Deaf people, but to society generally?

◀ Reading
You should now read Article 3.3 'Surdophrenia' by Terje Basilier in Reader Two. ◀

If we look closely at what Basilier says in the main text of his article a somewhat complex picture is revealed. Basilier discusses the importance of language learning for personality development and suggests that deaf children denied the use of sign language at school could face a serious crisis—the overemphasis on verbal language and a suppression of manual language in the classroom can create conflict in every area of the child's life and produce feelings of guilt and shame. He says: 'From these reflections it should be legitimate to ask whether it is the hearing loss *per se* or the multidimensional influences that follow with deafness which give the deaf person special characteristics'. Levine (1956) described such personality traits as impulsiveness, suggestibility, irritability and egocentricity. Myklebust (1960) states that early profound deafness imposes a restriction on the development of the personality. Basilier, however, claims that hearing people contribute to the manifestation of particular personality traits in deaf people because hearing people 'represent their handicap'; that is, communication becomes a significant problem between hearing people and deaf people because of the lack of understanding on the part of the hearing population.

From these examples it is possible to conclude either that the mere presence of early profound deafness itself produces a specific personality structure, or that the particular personality traits exhibited by deaf people are determined environmentally. But does this debate also allow for the possibility that a characteristic personality structure in profoundly Deaf people may not exist? Although the use of the word 'may' in the first quotation from Basilier above might indeed allow for this possibility, it is as if by naming the condition—surdophrenia, or Deaf Mind—Basilier has in fact made it real.

Furthermore, even though some of the earlier references to typical personality structures in deaf people originated in the early 1960s, they still form the basis of the popular notion of the profoundly Deaf person. This, together with the incurability and untreatability of early profound deafness, produces the response from the medical field. The scientific knowledge base of medicine offers little to the treatment of the physical aspects of deafness, but the values of society contribute to the medical treatment of Deaf people with social problems—the deafness itself is untreatable, so the presenting problems must be reframed as 'sickness' so that 'treatment' can be given.

Thus, the label of surdophrenia is applied like a medical diagnosis, and consequent 'treatment' offered, even though Basilier, for example, stresses the importance of environmental factors in the observation of special personality traits in deaf people, and Denmark reports that: '... it is suggested that the maturational retardation of the deaf might be alleviated by the use of combined methods of communication in the school and the home and by more realistic parent guidance and counselling' (Denmark, 1972). Denmark and Warren (1972) have observed that: 'These patients derive great benefit from the therapeutic environment, and especially from individual and group therapy, which enables them to gain insight into their problems and to develop increased social maturity'.

Generally, the 'problems' experienced by Deaf people are assumed to be a direct result of their deafness, and the solution given is to help Deaf people to adapt. An essential ingredient of this 'adapting' is what Denmark and Warren refer to as the ability of Deaf people 'to gain insight' into their problems. Myklebust makes this point even more clearly: 'The naivete of the deaf cannot be taken as an indication of a better emotional well-being. On the contrary those who stated that deafness was no handicap, those who showed the least understanding of what it means to hear, were the most disturbed' (Myklebust, 1960). The assumption that underpins this amazing piece of deduction is this: if you are profoundly deaf you must have psychological problems, if you say you do not have psychological problems, that is denial which is in itself a psychological problem. However, if you are profoundly deaf and you accept that because you are deaf you must have psychological problems, then you are believed, and you can have 'treatment' (for surdophrenia?). You may also be labelled as 'mentally unstable' and therefore regarded as unsuitable for 'normal' employment or education.

4 Stereotypes and social categories

The idea that certain groups of people display particular characteristics or personality traits is not, of course, confined to the medical profession. The way that Deaf people are represented in the media, as discussed in Unit 1, demonstrates a very narrow, and usually negative, view of deafness. And in Unit 4 each of the groups interviewed had features ascribed to it by other people. So, for example, the way that white people in Britain talk about Black people is often informed by notions of racial superiority and fears of being 'swamped' by immigrants; the way that heterosexual people talk about gay men and lesbians is to refer to them often as being 'unnatural', contrary to religious and moral codes, and dangerous to children.

The characteristics that are identified in a group of people are seen as specific to that group, and those who express such views do so in the belief that those characteristics arise as a consequence of belonging to that group. An example of this is the way that, within English society, Irish people are generally thought to be unintelligent and 'uncultured'. This stereotype is then applied to the whole Irish race, and any intelligent Irish people are simply viewed as individual exceptions and thus do not serve to contradict the stereotype. Social categorizing is a subject addressed by Potter and Wetherell, in *Discourse and Social Psychology*, in which they state:

> Categorization is an important and pervasive part of people's discourse. In the course of conversation everyone populates their lives with friends, doctors, Americans, extraverts, immigrants, and a thesaurus of other categories of people. Pick up any newspaper and many of the stories will concern people who are described, evaluated and understood not in terms of any unique features of their biography but through their category membership: 'model reveals star's secret life', 'wife found murdered'.
>
> (Potter and Wetherell, 1987)

A discourse is a way of talking or writing about something or someone, based upon a collection of beliefs, 'truths', myths, and the language that is used, to generate and underpin particular theoretical, political, or social positions. Using this approach, language is held to be a constructor of meaning as well as a reflection of reality. Potter and Wetherell write that social categories are not preformed and enduring entities, but that the formulation of social categories in discursive accounts is selective, designed to achieve certain aims. It is by analysing the accounts that we trace certain features which imply a legitimate action. For example, the people killed by Chinese soldiers in Tiananmen Square in June 1989, were described by the Western press as 'students', and by the government of China as 'criminals and counter-revolutionaries'. Both were describing the same group of people, who may, or may not, have been all of the things they were described to be. Discourse is constructed to accomplish certain goals: in the instance of Tiananmen Square, the goals of the Western press on the one hand, and of the government of China on the other, are clearly demonstrated in their respective modes of discourse.

Only by discourse analysis, according to Potter and Wetherell, can we account for inconsistent and sometimes contradictory accounts of social groups. They refer to a study of discursive accounts of Maoris by white middle-class New Zealanders (Wetherell *et al.*, in Potter and Wetherell, 1987). The study revealed many contradictory ways of describing Maori people, including that they are lazy/they are hard working, they are proud/they have lost their pride, they respect their older folk/they take advantage of their old.

Rack has also commented on this in relation to Afro-Caribbean people:

> The extravert ebullience of Afro-Caribbean people is a racial stereotype which draws support from loud music at late night parties, public carnivals, and back slapping joviality. Somehow the image of Caribbean islanders as good-natured, easy going and indolent people who take nothing seriously except cricket, co-exists with the image of violent angry aggressiveness and criminality in Britain: but stereotypes do not have to be logical.
>
> (Rack, 1982)

The contradictory nature of accounts such as these indicate, according to Potter and Wetherell, that psychology's traditional notions of fixed and enduring social categories should be replaced with a discourse analysis approach which emphasizes the idea that social categories are actively constructed through discursive accounts for different reasons and to achieve a range of aims.

Let us now reflect upon some of the views expressed about Deaf people by hearing people. Levine (1956) describes the kind of personality traits mentioned in Section 3 as emotional immaturity, personality constriction, and deficient emotional acceptability. Rainer and Altshuler (1967) claim that many Deaf people are egocentric, rigid, impulsive, and lacking in insight. And Denmark (1972) describes Deaf people as having invariably immature, egocentric, labile or explosive personalities. Now let us contrast these views with some views of Deaf people about themselves.

In 1989 the Council for the Advancement of Communication with Deaf People (CACDP) ran a series of courses in various parts of the country to train Deaf people as assessors for the Stage I Communication Skills Certificate. The training included a session on professionalism and impartiality. In this, the Deaf assessors looked at the concept of stereotyping, at strategies for identifying their own stereotyping and at developing ways to lessen the likelihood that stereotypes would influence examination assessment.

When asked to describe Deaf people and their behaviour, the Deaf assessors found it difficult, saying that Deaf people were all different, had many diverse characteristics and behaved in a variety of ways. They did not describe Deaf people in the way that Levine, Rainer and Altshuler, or Denmark had.

Not only is there clearly a difference of opinion about what Deaf people are like, there is also an issue about where power lies. Whilst the Deaf CACDP assessors have a certain amount of power over the people they are assessing, that power is largely given and mediated by hearing people and the organizational constraints of the CACDP. The power possessed by commentators such as Levine *et al.* is of a different order. As prominent figures in the study of deafness, they have a widespread influence based upon their professional status and qualifications. Their opinions are reinforced by their professional practice and clinical research. In other words, they are scientists, and science in modern society has a privileged position in verifying 'truth' and 'knowledge'.

Now consider the views of the same group of Deaf people about hearing people. The Deaf CACDP assessors were formed into small groups with the task of brainstorming images of hearing people. Participants were asked to record short descriptions of hearing people in response to questions such as, 'Tell me about hearing people. What are they like? How did they behave towards you/towards Deaf people?'. Most of the traits attributed to hearing people could be seen as negative. Only one small group spontaneously included a positive trait ('helpful'). One other group began to be concerned about not having listed anything positive after they had been working on the task for some time. This concern seems to have been triggered by thinking about the hearing trainers present and how they might be hurt or offended by all the negative remarks, so they added 'help with telephone' and 'calm'.

Here is a representative list of examples of the way the Deaf CACDP assessors described hearing people:

△   bossy

△   don't share

△   gossipy

△   ridicule or tease Deaf people

△   freeze when touched

△   stupid

△   selfish

△   insensitive

△   forgetful

△   lack flexibility

△   domineering

△   impatient

△   deceitful

△   stubborn

△   discriminate against Deaf people

△   nervous

△   withdrawn

△   embarrassed

△   fear physical contact

△   foolish

ITQ

Do you consider any of these views to be accurate? Or offensive? Are they reasonable? Or misinformed? If you are a hearing person, do you identify with the comments made about you? If you are a Deaf person, do you support any of the views expressed? Make a note of your response to the views expressed by:

(a) hearing professionals on Deaf people;

(b) Deaf people on themselves;

(c) Deaf people on hearing people.

Now jot down what you think may have been the aim of, and the influences on, choosing that particular way of talking/writing/commenting.

5 Summary of Sections 1 to 4

So far in this unit we have given some information about the psychiatric services available to deaf people, and have raised the question, 'Why are the majority of residents in the two specialist hospitals receiving in-patient care when they are classified as having a "behavioural disorder"?' We have suggested that the reasons for this are complex and not immediately apparent—a lack of resources for after-care is certainly a problem, for example, but it does not explain why these people are in a psychiatric hospital in the first place.

We suggest that a more productive line of enquiry is to analyse the structures of the mental health system. This reveals the influence of the medical model which encourages doctors to develop particular forms of professional behaviour. It also reveals the notion of deafness as a 'sickness', a disability—a direct contrast to the idea that Deaf people are a minority group with a discrete culture and language, a view put forward in the early units of this course. In addition, the diagnostic label of 'surdophrenia' is applied to some Deaf people who, it is claimed, demonstrate particular personality characteristics.

We have also seen that traditional notions of stereotyping and social categorization claim to identify actual and reliable features within certain social groups. We have suggested that discourse analysis demonstrates how different 'realities' are constructed through different ways of talking/writing/commenting.

6 The development of the mental sciences

In this section we will identify some of the features that characterize the development of the 'mental sciences' (psychology and psychiatry). It is important to discuss this here because in Section 7 we will be dealing with the way that psychological tests have been used with Deaf people, and an understanding of some of the more general issues will make that task easier. In this section we make reference only to those aspects of the development of the mental sciences that are directly relevant to the issues in this unit.[1]

As we stated in the Introduction, this unit is concerned with looking at the behaviour and practice of professionals in the mental health system, and not at Deaf people themselves. With that in mind, we will now focus upon the professionals responsible for the views expressed in Section 4. If we wished to categorize these professionals, we would say they belong to a group of people involved in the 'mental sciences' (psychology and psychiatry), and would add that the influence on society of the mental sciences has been significant, with many of the concepts and views enmeshed in wider debates and discourses on everyday life.

[1] Students wishing to further their understanding of this area are advised to read in the original the texts referred to in this section (this is not required reading for this course).

Psychology and psychiatry during the twentieth century have been characterized by notions of individualization and normalization. In this section we will look at how these notions relate to issues of social control, and in Section 7 the part they play in the way that Deaf people are dealt with in the mental health system.

In *Discipline and Punish*, Michel Foucault (1979) describes the birth of the modern prison system in the early nineteenth century, and a move away from public torture and public execution towards a more disciplining environment. Foucault saw this as a shift in focus from the 'body' of the offender to the 'mind' of the offender. Prison became a place where not only was liberty curtailed but prisoners were observed, scrutinized and individualized. They became 'knowable' through their biographical details, their instincts, their behaviour patterns and their personality traits. This construction of individual prisoners first of all identifies them as deviant and then provides the basis for their 'normalization' and for their return to society.

The techniques that Foucault identifies in the prison system are not exclusive to that domain. Workhouses, orphanages and charitable organizations concerned with moral rectitude all employed the disciplining techniques of observation, individualization and the gathering of specific information in order to compile a 'knowledge' base. Foucault calls this network a 'carcerel network' and claims that, by spreading the disciplining techniques throughout the network, the concepts of 'individualizing' and 'normalizing' became the currency of wider society rather than just of the penal system:

> The practice of placing individuals under 'observation' is a natural extension of a justice imbued with disciplinary methods and examination procedures. Is it surprising that the cellular prison, with its regular chronologies, forced labour, its authorities of surveillance and registration, its experts in normality, who continue and multiply the functions of the judge, should have become the modern instrument of penalty? Is it surprising that prisons resemble factories, schools, barracks, hospitals, which all resemble prisons?
>
> (Foucault, 1979)

Rose (1989) cites individualization as the organizing principle around which psychology developed as a discrete scientific discipline. Rose argues that a major function of the mental sciences is to 'discipline difference'; that is, that human beings are described, classified and managed through a process that focuses upon their individual characteristics. In this respect the mental sciences differ from other sciences in that the basic tools of the mental sciences (observation and notions of what is 'normal' and 'not normal') are initially the product of institutions within society; they are then established within the scientific programme and used to categorize the different elements of society. Psychologists are required to assess individuals for particular purposes—employment, education, health and welfare, and the justice system—and the precise nature of this assessment is determined by the reason for which it is being undertaken. For example, an educational psychologist tests children in relation to their academic and social activities within school, whereas a psychologist in the army tests individuals in relation to their suitability to become soldiers.

The task for early psychologists, according to Rose, was to find some way to mark differences. Whereas medical practitioners concerned with physiognomy were able to identify aberrations on the surface of the body, aberrations in the mind presented a different problem. A solution was the 'normal curve' first used by Francis Galton in 1883, originally devised for the categorization of 'normal' physical growth in children. Prior to this, ideas about what constituted 'normal' or average growth in children had been subjective. The development of a graph (the 'normal curve') meant that a child's growth rate could be mapped out to see how it compared with the average (the growth rate of the majority of children). This idea was then borrowed and used to compare information about the behaviour of individuals. Now statistical data collected by psychologists could be applied to a simple scale or graph, and deviations noted. The test itself became the epitome of individualization—once the data had rendered an aggregate of characteristics that established the 'normal' curve within the area of interest, then the test could simply be applied to any individual. Psychological tests and scales used with Deaf people are the focus of Section 7.

This simple technology used in psychological assessments has reduced human beings to calculable, quantifiable and manageable entities. By employing graphs and scales, previously unknown human variables have become visible and predictable. But in Rose's opinion the technology and language of the mental sciences have constructed, and not simply reflected, ideas of human reality. He states that: 'Increasingly in our own century psychology has participated in the development of regulatory practices which operated not by crushing subjectivity but by producing it, shaping it, modelling it, seeking to construct citizens committed to a personal identity, a moral responsibility and a social solidarity' (Rose, 1989).

7 Psychology, psychometrics and Deaf people

Psychology is concerned with the study of behaviour, and the study of the mind, and psychometrics provides a way of measuring psychological characteristics: it is 'mental testing'. This is usually achieved through the use of questionnaires or inventories. These include intelligence tests, creativity tests, and a whole battery of other tests, and are often used for personnel selection and vocational guidance. In this section we will consider the use of psychometric tests with Deaf people by looking at the results of one such study, *A Word in Deaf Ears*, and comparing this with an article by Harlan Lane in Reader Two, in which Lane is critical of such endeavours.

◀ Reading
At this point you should read Article 3.4 'Is there a "Psychology of the Deaf"?' by Harlan Lane in Reader Two. ◀

In his article, Lane states very clearly that he believes there is no such thing as a 'psychology of the Deaf'. He also speculates that investigations into such a concept may produce rather than reflect 'the perceived incompetence of deaf people'.

ITQ

Lane asserts that there can be no 'psychology of the Deaf'. Does this conflict with saying that Deaf people have a discrete culture that is different from hearing cultures? Write down your initial responses to this question.

◀ Comment

Keep your responses brief, such as a list of points. The object of the exercise is to encourage you to query new information and new theories rather than simply accept them or work from assumptions. You may wish to re-read Section 4 of this unit before writing your answer. ◀

We will now look at a research programme, entitled *A Word in Deaf Ears*, concerned with personality characteristics of deaf people. This was undertaken by Denmark *et al.* in 1979, and at the time of writing was the most recent British study of its kind.

This study is subtitled 'A Study of Communication and Behaviour in a Sample of Seventy-Five Deaf Adolescents', and was undertaken jointly by the Department of Psychiatry for the Deaf, Whittingham Hospital, Preston, and the Social Research Branch of the then Department of Health and Social Security (DHSS).[2]

Nine separate instruments are used in the study, including a battery of four educational, intellectual and psychological tests. We will refer to Lane's article in Reader Two, especially to the areas he identifies as being serious 'flaws'. You will need Lane's article with you as you work through this section.

7.1 Test administration and language

Lane argues that a major difficulty in testing Deaf people is that they may be unfamiliar with the formal procedures of psychological testing, and that this disadvantages them in comparison with hearing people. The apparatus of psychological testing is standardized on hearing people and does not fit easily with Deaf people. Lane also argues that, in order to test Deaf people appropriately, researchers must be familiar with Deaf culture—'they must turn to the Deaf community for advisers and collaborators in research design and implementation, for assistance in data collection and analysis, and for guidance in interpretation of results' (Lane, 1988).

It is made clear in *A Word in Deaf Ears* that 'only social workers with a high degree of skill in manual communication were involved'. And, whilst we are not told to what extent the social workers were familiar with Deaf culture,

---

[2]It could be argued that this study is now rather old, and perhaps no longer relevant. However, Michael Rodda (one of the authors of the study) used the findings of the study as the basic data for a further study he undertook with Denmark and Grove in 1981 (in Rodda and Grove, 1987). And, in Rodda's publication *Language, Cognition and Deafness* (Rodda and Grove, 1987) he refers to both previous studies in some detail in support of the notion of surdophrenia.

it does appear that an attempt has been made to overcome potential communication difficulties between the interviewers and the deaf subjects. However, only one of the four psychometric tests used in the study was designed for deaf subjects and its usefulness here may be in some doubt:

> The results achieved by both groups of adolescents on this test were remarkably poor even for deaf subjects ... In 1977, Montgomery had produced a mean score of 10.7 for a group of 53 profoundly deaf Scottish adolescents aged between 16 years and 16 years 6 months, which should be compared to the mean score of 8.2 obtained by the profoundly deaf adolescents in the sample.
>
> (Denmark *et al.*, 1979)

7.2 Test scoring

Subjectivity within tests has a disproportionate influence upon the results, according to Lane, and most studies fail to account for the problem of bias. A major plank of the study *A Word in Deaf Ears* was the Behaviour Rating Scale—the parents of all the subjects in the study were asked about any aspects of their child's behaviour which had given them cause for concern, and which they believed to be directly related to their child's deafness. Lane is quite clear in his article that he considers information gathered in this way to contain an unacceptably high level of bias. This test revealed a high incidence of reported problems which parents considered to be related to deafness. High on the list were: temper and aggression; easily led by bad company; major delinquency, and criminal activities; and being withdrawn.

The Behaviour Rating Scale was based on the Parents Interview Schedule, which constituted one interview with the parents (predominantly the mother). The Parents Interview Schedule was piloted on twenty families. However, the families were all chosen by schools for deaf children as being co-operative; the subjects were slightly older than the subjects in the study, they had higher academic achievements than would be expected, and they were all 'well adjusted'.

In the study, the comments of the parents about their children are taken as given, and used to support findings from other elements of the study. Could the results be, as Lane argues, a consequence of chance and error? And is Lane correct when he implies that because of the extra emotional stress on parents it is unreasonable to have confidence in their assessments of disturbance and maladjustment?

7.3 Test content and norms

Personality tests, Lane argues, are clearly designed for use with hearing people, so the practical application of these tests to Deaf people is inappropriate and often confusing to the Deaf person. Similarly, Lane states that, when the data are being interpreted, personality tests are designed to measure personality deviance in hearing people, and Deaf people will therefore compare poorly in these tests.

Of the four psychometric tests used in *A Word in Deaf Ears*, one (the Four Rules Test) was designed specifically for use with deaf subjects but returned remarkably poor results; one (the Snijders Oomen Test), although designed for hearing subjects, had been well validated on Deaf subjects but only a very small part of it was used; another (the Gibson Spiral Maze Test) was viewed as unproblematic because, even though it was designed for hearing subjects, the test was non-verbal; and the fourth (the Gates MacGinitie Test) was designed for American primary school children and had not been standardized on Deaf or British subjects.

It could be argued, as Lane does, that it is inappropriate to administer such tests to Deaf subjects as they will probably compare poorly with hearing subjects; that the norms for Deaf people and hearing people are different, are culturally determined, and that, therefore, the results and their interpretations are contentious and could be misleading.

7.4 Subject populations

Lane's final criticism is that the research treats Deaf people as if they were a homogeneous group and fails to account for differences. Failure to take differences into account creates two major problems. First, trends that are identified from the research cannot be confidently stated to be purely as a result of deafness. Second, it is not possible to state to which other populations these trends may apply.

The sample group in *A Word in Deaf Ears* was subject to eight conditions. They had to have:

1   Attended a school designated for deaf children.
2   Left school during 1973 or 1974.
3   A hearing impairment of no later than 2 years of age of onset.
4   Entered a school for the deaf before the age of 6 years.
5   No additional handicaps, either physical or mental.
6   Parents without significant hearing loss.
7   Parents whose mother tongue was English.
8   One or more natural parent or substitute parent who had known the respondent since birth.

Of the original seventy-five adolescents in the sample group, forty were male and thirty-five were female. Information was also gathered about the size of families they came from, their position in the family, whether they had any hearing impaired siblings, the marital status of parents at the time of the interview, and socio-economic groupings of the families.

Following this, all subjects were given a functional hearing test and it was discovered that only forty-three out of the seventy-five could be considered profoundly deaf, the others being deemed partially hearing, and the original group was divided into these two smaller sub-groups. However, none of the already gathered information was transferred into the new groupings, so it is not possible to know from the study how many of the profoundly Deaf group were male/female, or any information about the spread of family backgrounds amongst each group. Neither are we given any information about ethnicity. We cannot assume that those people for whom English is the 'mother tongue' are white British—they may be, for example, Black British, Irish, Christian Asian or Gypsies.

Lane concludes by stating that there is no 'psychology of the Deaf', and that there should not be one, any more than there should be a psychology of Black people or Mexican-Americans. In testing Deaf people, researchers merely reinforce their own stereotypes and add to the oppression of Deaf people by locating the problem with them rather than with the hearing majority.

◀ Activity 2 and Reading

Now look at the last section again, referring both to the study *A Word in Deaf Ears* and to Harlan Lane's article in Reader Two. Which of Lane's criticisms of attempts to develop a 'psychology of the Deaf' apply most to Denmark's study? Make some notes on this, and then write some brief notes on why you think this particular study (*A Word in Deaf Ears*) may have been constructed in this way, and what factors have contributed to its findings.

The following two articles in Reader Two may help you—both address issues of psychological perspectives and deaf people:

Article 3.1, 'Cognition and Language' by Stephen Quigley and Peter Paul;

Article 3.2, 'Looking for Meaning in Sign Language Sentences' by Jim Kyle. ◀

8 Summary of Sections 6 and 7

We have looked at the way the development of the mental sciences has encouraged a process of the marking and regulation of individual differences, and notions of 'normal' and 'not normal', which disadvantage Deaf people.

We used the study *A Word in Deaf Ears* to illustrate some of these points and to examine the validity of Lane's criticisms of attempts to establish a 'psychology of the Deaf'. Mainstream psychology has changed significantly since the mid-1970s, and psychometric testing is a rapidly diminishing feature. Lane's comments, therefore, would appear to be dated. However, in the Deaf field, the idea that early profound deafness produces a particular personality type still seems as strong as ever. Results of psychometric tests carried out in 1979, and opinions cast as long ago as 1948, continue to be presented as evidence to support the notion of surdophrenia (Rodda and Grove, 1987). Why is this so? Parker writes:

> The efforts of experimental social psychology to break the mental processes of individuals into measurable and manipulable components can be seen as part of the power pattern of contemporary society. Foucault's work could only reinforce the opposition to positivism and individualism that characterizes the 'old paradigm'. At the same time, what is sometimes described as the shift within the discipline of psychology away from obsessive quantification has to be linked with intellectual, social and political changes outside, changes in the discourse of the social world.

> (Parker, 1989)

This would suggest that the treatment of Deaf people in the mental health system is determined by the current views about them, not only those of psychiatric personnel, but also in the fields of medicine and education, social work, and publicly through the media.

In the next section we will look more closely at the process of the mental health system, and the way it operates around Deaf people.

9 The development of the British mental health system

The origins of the modern mental health system in the UK can be traced back to the early part of the nineteenth century. Precisely which event actually heralded the birth of this new 'system' is determined by one's view of *why* it developed, rather than *how* it developed.

In Section 6 the views of Foucault and Rose were presented on how and why the mental sciences developed. In particular, these authors focus on why early scientists became concerned with the notion of 'normality' and therefore with what was 'not normal'. This is one view that might help to explain the development of mental health both as a service to patients and also as a basis for a new professional breed.

Some authors (e.g. Scull, 1977) focus their explanation on the role of the economy and its influence on social policy. This is a theme that will appear again in this part of the unit. Let us therefore look briefly at the major events which can be said to be significant in the development of the social policy of British mental health services.

Most of the early legislation was not concerned with the welfare of the insane but rather with the control of the property of 'lunatics', and with them being a danger or annoyance to others. The County Asylums Act of 1808 then brought a major shift in direction. This was a significant piece of legislation because it transferred the responsibility of incarcerating 'lunatics' from the private sector to County Authorities. Up to that point, patients were held exclusively in private, fee-paying institutions and the standards of care led to much public concern. The County Asylums Act of 1808 guaranteed two things:

1   A significant number of patients under state control, who would become available for medical investigation.

2   A requirement for the recruitment of medical practitioners specializing with mental patients.

The year 1841 could be seen as a milestone in the development of the British mental health system as it saw the establishment of the Association of 'Medical Officers of Asylums and Hospitals for the Insane'. That event consolidated the emergence of psychiatry as a clearly definable discipline within the medical profession. There were parallel movements in Germany and America at around the same time.

These events in themselves do not fully explain why the mental health system developed as it did, yet they appear to be significant. The development of the mental sciences, and the professionalization of the medical practitioners are also important factors. Just as surgeons needed bodies on which to practise and develop their surgical skills, so those medical practitioners with mental patients required access to patients with whom they could experiment and develop their treatment programmes.

Practitioners in the field also required recognition and credibility. Madness and magic were closely linked throughout Europe up until the seventeenth century, and old beliefs were hard to dispel, despite the more 'scientific' explanations of madness that were beginning to appear. The fact that major public figures are not immune to periods of mental ill-health is bound to raise the level of interest of the general public, as witnessed in 1987 by the amount of media attention paid to the two members of the Royal family who had spent a considerable part of their lives in an institution. The impact of such a situation in the eighteenth century would have been more sensational:

> King George the Third delivers his 'my lords, ladies and peacocks' oration to the opening of Parliament and is whisked off to be bled, blistered, strait-jacketed, knocked about, dosed with bark and saline, confined to Windsor Castle, and publicly debated in pamphlet and Parliamentary Committee—an airing which, while of doubtful benefit to His Majesty, assisted in the establishment of psychiatry as a recognised medical profession. The mental illness and psychiatric confinements of Christopher Smart and William Cowper, and later of the Marquis de Sade and John Clare, effect a powerful charge of sympathy from the literary public to the plight of asylum inmates.
>
> (Sedgwick, 1982)

The 1980s will be remembered as a decade of the community care debate; that is, debate about whether people are best served as patients within institutions or within their locality. Services for both deaf and hearing people have seen major developments since the Second World War. Earlier in this section we said that some authors feel that both quality and quantity of service is very much linked to the economy and, therefore, to those who influence it—for example, the government, the City and powerful organizations such as the Trades Union Congress (TUC), the Confederation of British Industry (CBI) and major political parties.

Let us examine the ideas of Andrew Scull at this point in order to determine just how the economy might affect services to Deaf people.

Scull postulates '... a more intensive exploitation of the labor of the domestic population' as a major reason for the establishment and development of the state-controlled asylum system. Capitalist enterprise requires the regulation of cheap, or free, labour. Deviant groups such as '... vagrants, minor criminals, prostitutes, paupers, beggers, lunatics, orphans, and so forth represented those most readily subjected to state control' (Scull, 1977).

Scull suggests that within western capitalist states welfare provision is at the mercy of market forces, therefore during times of economic decline expensive resources such as institutions begin to lose their funding in favour of 'supposedly' cheaper community-based services. This view is challenged by Peter Sedgwick (1982), who claims that it is implausible to argue that the state of the national economy will determine specific policy regarding the treatment of mental patients, in isolation from the other factors. Sedgwick offers an explanation (also partially consistent with the views of Scull and Foucault) that changes in the mental health system must be consistent with general developments in welfare provision in order to be feasible. For example, the granting of outdoor relief for mental patients in the nineteenth century would have raised serious questions about the plight of other beleaguered groups refused such help.

ITQ

Does Scull's analysis hold true for the development of psychiatric services for Deaf people? Refer back to Section 1 on the provision of psychiatric services. Make notes on this before proceeding.

In Section 1 we said that the first psychiatric unit was set up in 1968 at Whittingham Hospital near Preston, under the aegis of Dr John Denmark, and that the second was set up in London, in 1974, based at Springfield Hospital. Nowadays Springfield is a large and expanding institutional and community-based resource. The years between 1968 and 1974, when both the Whittingham and Springfield Hospitals were set up, were said to be times of expansion, both of statutory services and within the private sector. But what has happened since?

Since 1977, when the then Labour Government began to cut welfare funding in general, provision for Deaf people has remained relatively unscathed. In fact, in London services grew steadily during the 1980s. It would be fair to say that the expansion of psychiatric services during this period was community based rather than institutional, but is it simply a case of economics? Another contributory factor might be changing work practices and shifts in ethos that lead to community provision, as suggested by Sedgwick (1982). In Section 13 we will look at the proposed changes from institutional care in favour of a more community-based service which began to develop the 1980s and we will return to examine the role of the economy as a motivating factor relating to psychiatric services.

Having looked at how psychiatric services developed and at their relationship with the state and economy, we move on in Section 10 to look at the process of gaining access to the limited resources available to Deaf people.

◀ Video

Now watch Video Three. Pay special attention to the experiences of Kim, Michael and Lorna. What do they say about gaining access to services? ◀

10 The mental health system: the process

The mental health system is not merely the bricks and mortar of the various institutions that comprise it, but the relationships created between the plethora of professionals and the patients they serve. Who are these professionals and what do they do?

We do not have sufficient space within this unit to give an account of the roles of the various professionals employed by the NHS psychiatric services, though a brief explanation may help you to understand better some of the information contained in Video Three, as well as within this unit.

We have divided general psychiatric services into three main categories:

1   Psychiatric provision for the criminally insane, such as Rampton, Moss Side and Broadmoor.
2   Hospital-based services which may be as in-patient or out-patient. In-patient care may be in a special psychiatric hospital such as the Maudsley or Friern Barnet Hospitals, or as a department within a large general hospital. Out-patient care is very diverse, it can be based within either a general or a psychiatric hospital or within the community (e.g. in a day centre), or perhaps as a residential facility attached to a hospital (e.g. Hugenot Place which is attached to Springfield Hospital).
3   Community nursing which in general treats patients in their own homes.

It would be simplistic to say that psychiatrists prescribe one or other of these options because generally patients are cared for in two or more settings; for example, as a hospital out-patient with day centre care and community nursing.

Each psychiatric facility is headed by a consultant psychiatrist. The team may include one or more of the following: a psychologist, a junior psychiatrist, an occupational therapist, a counsellor, an educationalist, a psychotherapist and a social worker, as well as an assortment of nursing staff.

10.1 Referral

Access to psychiatric services, except in emergency situations, is through the general practitioner (GP) or family doctor. The GP is the key to the majority of hospital- or clinic-based services, whether in-patient or within the community. When a person presents with a potential psychiatric problem the GP will seek advice by referring him or her to a consultant psychiatrist. Consultants are almost exclusively hospital based and it is rare for them to see individuals in the community. The choice of service then is largely dependent upon factors such as the perspective of the consultant psychiatrist and the actual resources available.

Is this also the case for Deaf people? Or does the fact that there are so few resources for Deaf people and their specialized requirements affect the pattern and style of referral? There is certainly some anecdotal evidence from Social Workers with Deaf People (SWDP) that GPs and non-specialist consultant psychiatrists are reluctant to become involved with Deaf people suspected of being mentally ill, as the following two examples show:

> I sectioned X twice. He was admitted to the local psychiatric hospital, and both times he was discharged within twenty-four hours, and still in a terrible state. It gave me no chance to make any further arrangements. When I challenged the consultant about it I was told that because they didn't have the resources to offer him any proper treatment there was no point in keeping him in.
>
> (A Social Worker with Deaf People, 1989, personal communication)

> I was certain that she needed psychiatric help, and I'd taken her to her own GP so many times, and he had refused to refer for a psychiatric assessment, that my professional relationship with him deteriorated to such a point that it ceased to be useful for X. He refused to see me once he knew what I wanted, and on one occasion he was really abusive to me on the telephone. In the end X attacked an old woman on a bus and the police sectioned her. She told me she would do something if I didn't get her some help.
>
> (A Social Worker with Deaf People, 1989, personal communication)

ITQ

How do these accounts compare with Lorna's experience in Video Three?

Absence of specialist knowledge amongst GPs and psychiatrists may mean that their view of Deaf people is informed by general societal attitudes; that is, prejudicial and stereotyped. They will almost certainly have access to, or construct for themselves, a medical view of Deaf people. In Sections 3 and 4 we discussed the influence of the medical model and the development of the negative stereotypes attributed to Deaf people, and how the medical model, in turn, may continue to perpetuate these views by ascribing to Deaf people certain personality traits. The lack of awareness displayed by some doctors often may create obstacles at an early stage for Deaf people trying to gain access to services.

ITQ

Does Kim's story in Video Three support this statement?

In some cases both Whittingham and Springfield will accept referrals from non-medical personnel, such as Social Workers with Deaf People (who may also be 'approved social workers' (ASW) as defined by the Mental Health Act 1983). Could this apparent breach of protocol be as a result of difficulties experienced by using the conventional channels of patient referral?

ITQ

How might a referral from a specialist Social Worker with Deaf People be more effective than other referrals? Make notes on how this might benefit both the patient and receiving hospital.

It is certainly more likely that a Social Worker with Deaf People will be able to establish a more effective communication with a Deaf person than will a GP or a non-specialist psychiatrist; they may have more knowledge of specialist resources, and may have a greater understanding of the presenting problem. But is this the most appropriate way of dealing with problems of access?

In a paper in the *British Journal of Psychiatry*, Denmark (1985) describes a study of 250 patient referrals to the Whittingham Hospital. One hundred and fifty-nine were referred by Social Workers with Deaf People, fifty-seven by other consultants, three by GPs and two referred themselves. Referral direct from specialist social workers may improve access to services for some Deaf people, though the very low numbers of specialist social workers nationally may mean that some Deaf people will not have even this 'short-circuit' arrangement available to them.

Earlier in the unit we stated that the majority of in-patients in both Whittingham and Springfield were diagnosed as having a behavioural disorder and yet the mode of access to the rehabilitation services at both hospitals is the same as for mentally ill people in general. The independent specialist rehabilitation units will, in theory, accept direct referrals, but they do say that they prefer to have a psychiatric report.

10.2 Assessment

The origins of modern mental health legislation are found within the 1959 Mental Health Act which replaced all previous laws and regulations relating to mental illness and mental handicap. It incorporated an important principal, 'that no one should be admitted to hospital if care in the community was more appropriate'. 1976 saw the publication of the influential White Paper, *The Review of the Mental Health Act 1959*. Many of the proposals contained within the White Paper became law under the 1982 Mental Health (Amendment) Act. This Act introduced new powers relating to the treatment and discharge of mentally disordered patients. A consolidation bill was introduced at the time the 1982 Act received assent and it pulled together most of the post-war legislation into a single Act. This became the 1983 Mental Health Act which received assent on 9 May 1983.

Assessment under the 1983 Mental Health Act has a specific meaning. It refers to the compulsory admission of patients to hospital under Sections 2 and 4, for the purposes of assessment.

This is not what we are referring to here, however. The assessment we are referring to is the one that takes place before the patient is admitted, usually by an approved social worker (ASW) and at least one medical practitioner. (This will vary according to which section of the Act is being invoked.) There are two reasons why we emphasize this:

1   Assessment is the cornerstone of social work practice, a satisfactory assessment will lead to progressive case planning and appropriate service delivery.

2   There are some important issues to be considered when attempting to assess whether or not a Deaf person should be compulsorily admitted to a psychiatric hospital.

The 1983 Mental Health Act is organized around the principle of the 'least restrictive alternative'; that is, that hospitalization should only be the last resort when care in the community is no longer possible. Assessment interviews according to government regulations should be conducted 'in a suitable manner', the most immediate issue for Deaf people being that of communication. A Department of Health and Social Security circular in 1987 tried to clarify this area as '... taking into account any hearing or linguistic difficulties the patient may have'.[3]

One may view the emphasis of the then DHSS to be slightly oppressive, in that the problems related to hearing and language are assumed to be with the Deaf person. There is, at least, recognition in the Act of a communication issue to be addressed. What is not taken into account, however, is the question of Deaf culture, and the misunderstandings that can arise with hearing people when they attempt to make professional judgements about the behaviour of a Deaf person. You will be aware from working on this unit so far, and from earlier units, that there are many, and competing, views of Deaf people, and that the nature of any judgements made in a particular situation may vary enormously.

The fact that there are any references at all in the Act to Deaf people is down to persistent lobbying by organizations like the British Deaf Association (BDA). The BDA has published the following guidelines to assist in the best way possible the interviewing and assessment of Deaf people, taking into account both the national and local variations of personnel and resources. The BDA recommends that:

> 1 Wherever practicable those Specialist Social Workers with the Deaf employed by the local authority should be approved under the terms of the Mental Health Act 1983 and be called upon to interview a deaf person referred for possible admission to hospital. The BDA regards this as the most preferable arrangement.

> 2 If (1) above is not practicable, the Specialist Social Worker with the Deaf should be called upon to act as co-worker and to facilitate communication between the client and the Approved Social Worker.

> 3 Where the local authority does not employ Specialist Social Workers with the Deaf, arrangements with neighbouring local authorities or local voluntary agencies should be established to provide either of the arrangements (1 and 2 respectively) above.

> 4 If efforts to obtain the services of a Specialist Social Worker with the Deaf under the arrangements recommended (1, 2 and 3 above) are unsuccessful, a record of the attempts made to do so should be kept.

> 5 Where it does not prove possible to involve the Specialist Social Worker with Deaf at the point of referral, he/she should be involved as soon as possible afterwards as a co-worker.
> (British Deaf Association, 1984)

[3] For a fuller picture of the Mental Health Act 1983, refer to the *Legislation Booklet*.

The BDA guidelines appear to offer a clear list of alternatives. Yet difficulties may arise even where the approved social worker is also a Social Worker with Deaf People, particularly if known to the Deaf person being interviewed. What difficulties do you imagine might arise in this situation?

The BDA recommendations emphasize the importance of the contribution of the 'Specialist Social Worker with the Deaf' (SWDP). The problem here is that there is little agreement as to exactly what a Social Worker with Deaf People is, or the functions this person fulfils. In some areas, SWDPs are 'visitors' of Deaf people; in other areas they operate as community workers, or as local authority social workers with statutory powers, or simply as interpreters. The possibilities are many, and the mixture of roles and responsibilities can be confusing. You will find a more detailed discussion of the role of SWDPs when you come to Unit 7.

Added to this, SWDPs are not immune to subscribing to some of the stereotypes of Deaf people expressed in the early part of this unit and may, in fact, hold a view of Deaf people as having a particular personality type. The availability of SWDPs does not by itself necessarily lead to a 'fair' assessment.

There may be a number of problems for a Deaf person even before the assessment interview begins because of the whole range of assumptions that may be made about that person simply because he or she is deaf. The Social Worker with Deaf People will usually be the only professional present who can communicate with Deaf people, and this places the social worker in a very powerful position. Neither the Deaf person, nor other hearing professionals present, will have access to the whole of the discussion other than through the SWDP. If the Deaf person cannot understand the SWDP, he or she may be too anxious to complain or to ask for someone else. As Elliott *et al.* state:

> Defense against anxiety can affect the communication process with a deaf client just as it can with a hearing client. While such defenses may be expressed in similar ways, eg emotional blocking, perseveration, or echolalia, other defense behaviors are especially characteristic of deaf clients, eg signing rapidly to obscure meaning or nodding despite lack of understanding. Interruption of eye contact by a deaf client whose communication with the external world is visual is evidence of particular discomfort. It is often an aggressive defensive act or a hostile act, or it could be fatigue. It is the equivalent of hearing people putting their fingers in their ears.
>
> (Elliott *et al.*, 1987)

Deaf people in these situations may worry in case they are disadvantaged by asking for a different social worker, or that there is no-one else anyway; that they may be considered stupid or mad because they cannot understand the social worker; or that the social worker may be angry with them, and perhaps act against their best interests. The social worker may know the Deaf person well, so there is perhaps the danger of this other relationship being intrusive or affected.

So whilst the BDA are right to stress the importance of the involvement of the 'Specialist Social Worker with the Deaf', issues of power and access are still of primary significance. The involvement of an interpreter (or the use of a SWDP as an interpreter), may be even more problematic:

> Regretfully we are obliged to consider the use of interpreters, even though this reduces diagnostic precision very greatly, sometimes to the level of guess-work. The interpreter may be a member of the patient's own family or circle, or an outsider brought in for the purpose by the practitioner.
>
> Both have drawbacks ... under no circumstances should children be asked to interpret medical details for their parents. The practice is widespread and some writers have recommended it ... but it appears to us to be unethical, unprofessional, uncivilised, and totally unacceptable.
>
> (Rack, 1982)

Rack was referring to ethnic minorities, but the issues of language, culture, power and prejudice are just as relevant for the Deaf community. It is also not uncommon for hearing children to interpret for their Deaf parents, often in areas that they as children have neither experience nor understanding. Sadly, there have been cases of hearing children being used as interpreters in mental health assessment interviews of their own Deaf parents.

ITQ

Having seen Video Three, what benefit do you think could have been gained, if any, for Michael, Kim or Lorna, if an interpreter had been available? Make notes on this question before continuing.

10.3 Diagnosis

In the quotation at the beginning of Section 1, Denmark suggests that 'deaf people are no more likely to suffer from frank mental illness than the hearing population'. This begs the question, 'What is mental illness and who decides whether or not someone is mentally ill?'. As we said in the Introduction, there is no substantive agreement about the nature of mental illness and so the label, when applied to Deaf people, becomes even less tangible. Diagnosis of a psychiatric illness ultimately relies on the professional clinical judgement of the psychiatrist. Ingleby is critical of this method of diagnosis:

> Clinical judgement is a blank cheque which can be filled with any amount of tacit biases and unwritten rules, and completely undermines psychiatry's claim to be based on observations more solid than lay judgement. For the fact that clinical expertise is maintained by a professional clique is not, in itself, any guarantee of objectivity—more likely the reverse.
>
> (Ingleby, 1981)

Springfield and Whittingham Hospitals traditionally have each employed a different diagnostic approach. At Springfield each patient will be seen by a number of professionals in one day, including a psychiatrist, an occupational therapist, a psychologist, a nurse and a social worker. The diagnosis treatment plan is informed by the pooling of information. Whittingham adopts a more traditional diagnostic procedure, in that the patient is initially interviewed by the consultant psychiatrist who, as the 'responsible medical officer', formulates an initial diagnosis; later the patient can be seen by a variety of professionals and a treatment plan formulated. The style of admission and diagnosis in either hospital will vary significantly for individual patients, depending on the nature and urgency of their referral.

Timmermans' study in Belgium found that five out of seven deaf patients in a psychiatric hospital were detained as in-patients for a period exceeding 5 years (Timmermans, 1988). The situation in the UK appears to be equally serious for Deaf patients. Denmark (1966) found that the average length of stay in general psychiatric hospitals in Britain was over 20 years for deaf people. Denmark's findings were consistent with Timmermans' study in Belgium 20 years later!

Denmark's study identified misdiagnosis as part of the reason for the unacceptably lengthy periods of detainment. In only five out of twenty-eight cases did he agree with the original diagnosis and he found no signs of subnormality despite this being the diagnostic label for nearly half of the referrals! Diagnostic practice, as with notions of mental illness, is vulnerable to misinterpretation and, as Ingleby commented, is more likely to be subjective than objective, whether patients are hearing or deaf.

Rodda and Grove's study (Rodda and Grove, 1987) raises an interesting point. Do Deaf people from different countries suffer from the same mental illnesses or is the apparent discrepancy in diagnosis based on other factors? Rodda and Grove express concern that, in studies they looked at, Danish people were the only ones to suffer from paranoia: in fact it was a label given to 20 per cent of deaf psychiatric patients. In contrast, half of the admissions in the UK and USA are labelled as schizophrenic.

According to Rodda and Grove, it is in the 'hodgepodge class of behavioural disorders' that there is consistency of diagnosis. These initial 'behavioural disorder' labels were essentially applied to referrals from teachers, social workers, psychologists, parents and others. Rodda and Grove ask, 'Do the data mean that the specialised knowledge of psychiatrists lead to professional inconsistencies and the ignorance of teachers is bliss?' (Rodda and Grove, 1987). As with mental illness, there is no widely accepted definition of behavioural disorder.

ITQ

At the beginning of the unit you were asked to account for and explain why Deaf people spend disproportionally longer periods in psychiatric hospitals than do hearing people. Reading through your notes and what you have read so far, how would you now explain the apparent lack of consistency in diagnosis?

◀ Comment
The issues of language, culture, power and prejudice, to which we have referred throughout this unit, may also apply here. Moraitis raises very similar issues in his description of the problems faced by ethnic minorities in Australia (Moraitis, 1979). He is concerned at the ever-increasing rates of mental illness being diagnosed amongst Australia's non-English speaking immigrant population, and the apparent inability of the Australian mental health system to help them. He locates the reasons in communication difficulties, cultural misunderstanding, and the view of the powerful white population that members of ethnic minority populations are second-class citizens. These issues are also relevant to Deaf people in the mental health system and may affect the way that diagnoses are formulated. ◀

◀ Video
Early in the unit it was clearly stated that the large majority of Deaf people who are resident as in-patients are classified as having a behavioural disorder. Denmark suggests misdiagnosis and Rodda puts forward the idea of inter-professional inconsistency, but perhaps the significant lack of resources is also an important factor. It may be useful to watch Video Three again, paying special attention to comments made about assessment, referral and diagnosis and how these personal accounts accord with the professional explanations of Denmark and Rodda. Make notes on how the experiences in Video Three may either confirm or reject the theoretical explanations. ◀

10.4 Treatment

It is important to understand what is meant by 'treatment'. As a term it has fallen into disrepute since the 1960s, with the development of 'anti-medical' and 'anti-psychiatry' movements. Whilst it is clearly medical in nature, its meaning is broad (if not imprecise), and it licenses a wide range of actions under the umbrella of appropriate medical activity.

The Mental Health Act 1983 makes no distinction between treatment and medical treatment. It states that treatment 'includes nursing, and also includes care, habilitation and rehabilitation under medical supervision'. This view of treatment is confirmed by Collins English Dictionary which defines treatment as '... the application of medicines, surgery, psychotherapy, etc. to a patient ... '.

In their 'Operational Policy' document, Whittingham Hospital explain that individual treatment programmes consist of: 'Individual and group therapy, occupational therapy, education, art therapy, speech therapy, social therapy, vocational training and physical methods of treatment', whilst Springfield's 'Operational Policy' document refers to: 'a full range of physical and psychological therapies including group, behaviour, social therapy and education'.

Springfield and Whittingham both retain the option of traditional treatments such as drug therapy, yet they appear to be more heavily committed to developing their rehabilitation programmes. In fact, Whittingham and Springfield are similar to the Hayfields Rehabilitation Unit in Scotland, in that all three have a small proportion of residents diagnosed as mentally ill; the rest are adults of low functional ability, mostly with severe behavioural problems. Where they differ significantly is that Hayfields is not a psychiatric hospital, does not directly employ medical staff, and is

Figure 6.3   A group session at Richardson House
(Source: courtesy of the Royal National Institute for the Deaf)

not part of the NHS. This raises interesting questions as to why the same 'clientele' should be at one time part of the medical paradigm and at other times not.

One of the most interesting contrasts between Springfield and Whittingham Hospitals is a philosophical one, centring around the issue of psychotherapy for Deaf people. Springfield have trained psychotherapists on their staff and actively employ psychotherapy as a strategy with some Deaf patients, whilst Whittingham reject psychotherapy as a viable treatment for use with Deaf people.

Classic psychotherapy relies upon a significant level of interpretive interaction between therapist and client. The aim is to bring about changes at the level of thought, emotion or behaviour, or any combination of the three. This interactive process allows the therapist to interpret the actions/thoughts/feelings expressed or displayed by the client. The interpretation is translated into active change in the patient through the development of greater self-awareness.

◀ Video

Having read our definition of psychotherapy, now re-watch Video Three. Whilst doing so, think about the following question: 'How does our definition of psychotherapy relate to what is happening with the group of patients from Springfield?' ◀

Psychotherapy has been disparagingly referred to as the 'talking treatment' (MIND, 1974), and has been the subject of much debate as to its efficiency, and also its place within the medical paradigm. Thomas Szasz has no difficulty, viewing it as a human relationship which is subject to certain specific precepts, with scant medical value, whilst Ellenberger asserts that psychotherapy is a direct development of primitive medicine and draws a line from exorcism, magnetism and hypnotism, to psychotherapy (Clare, 1980). Busfield (1986) points out that psychotherapy is rarely used in the treatment of psychotic patients. The use of psychotherapy within a psychiatric hospital is therefore contentious. So how appropriate is it in the treatment of Deaf people? Philip Rack raises serious doubts as to the value of psychotherapy except in specific circumstances: 'Psychotherapy of this kind may suit some highly educated subjects in individualistic and introspective societies, but it cannot be applied everywhere' (Rack, 1982).

The problem, according to Rack, is that psychotherapy does not take account of class, culture, or educational background. If this is so, it creates a major difficulty in the employment of psychotherapy with Deaf people generally, and more so specifically for those Deaf people within the British mental health system: generally, because psychotherapy is a development within the majority culture, and relies heavily on spoken language; and specifically, because the vast majority of Deaf people in the mental health system are regarded as 'maladjusted', 'socially immature' or 'behaviourally disturbed', so other forms of rehabilitation may appear to be more appropriate.

Rack is writing about ethnic minorities, but his points are pertinent to Deaf people. He states that, 'Even if we abandon strict Freudian concepts, the need for rapport and empathy remains, and these are most easily established when the two participants have life experiences and value systems in common' (Rack, 1982). Rack's statement would suggest that Deaf people would best be treated by other Deaf people. This is a point we will develop later in the unit.

Even if it were possible to overlook the cross-cultural and linguistic difficulties in a psychotherapeutic approach to the treatment of Deaf patients, there are still a number of factors which raise problems for all individual therapy models within psychiatric settings. First, the background is that of a hospital and the context is medical. The dominant discourse within medicine is that of sickness and cure, and it locates both the source of the problem and the object of treatment to be the individual. Changes need to be effected in the patient. Yet we know that the overwhelming majority of Deaf people within the specialist part of the system are not mentally ill in the conventional sense; rather, they are described as 'socially immature' or 'behaviourally disturbed'. We are told that this is largely as a result of environmental factors, particularly a lack of sign language in the education of Deaf people (Basilier, 1964a; Denmark, 1972). One therefore needs to ask how individual, medically based treatment can be either appropriate or recommended when, from the evidence we have, whatever form of help Deaf people receive should reflect their cultural and collective needs. Perhaps 'changes' could be made instead to those parts of the social system that produce their distress in the first place.

Second, there is the issue of the power relationship between therapist and client/patient. The health service, particularly the mental health system, generates discourses of power in society. The psychiatrist has legal and organizational power, and moral authority, and the patient is reliant on the psychiatrist as the 'expert'. Even if the psychiatrist wished to move from the position of being the provider of answers to that of an enabler (a necessary shift in a psychotherapeutic setting), this may not match the patient's expectations and therefore be met with resistance. This is particularly so in the case of Deaf people who, from their contact with teachers and social workers, are encouraged to be dependent upon professionals.

Can psychotherapy work at all with Deaf patients in a psychiatric hospital setting? We indicated earlier that psychotherapy requires a high level of functioning on behalf of the client/patient but it also requires another important ingredient, effective communication. At the time of writing, none of the psychotherapists employed within the health service has yet passed Stage III of the CACDP Communication Skills Certificate, which suggests that the interpretative function of the therapist must be significantly reduced. Nor can a qualified interpreter be used effectively as therapy requires the development of a 'relationship' between therapist and client, and this development would be significantly skewed by the presence of a third party.

11 Summary of Sections 9 and 10

In Section 9 we looked at the birth of the mental health system in Britain and saw that the event that actually heralded its inception was likely to be determined by one's view of *why* it developed, rather than *how* it developed. It clearly did not exist in any coherent form before the eighteenth century, and developed slowly within the private sector until the establishment of the National Health Service in 1948.

Changes to the focus of provision from incarceration to rehabilitation were presented, with different explanations. For example, Scull believes that economic considerations dictate the form of provision; that is, that in times of economic decline, funding is diverted to cheaper community-based services. This view is challenged by both Sedgwick and Busfield.

Section 10 dealt, in some length, with the mechanisms whereby Deaf patients are processed by the machinery of institutions and professionals within the mental health system. The usual way in which hearing people are referred to psychiatric services does not, on the whole, accord with the practice developed by specialist Social Workers with Deaf People.

Much of current social work practice is determined by the framework laid down by the 1983 Mental Health Act. It emphasizes the principle of the 'least restrictive alternative'. This appears to have little relevance to Deaf people because of the national paucity of choice for referral as shown in Section 1.

Denmark asserts that 'deaf people are no more likely to suffer from frank mental illness than the hearing population', and there appears to be very little evidence to contradict that. Yet misdiagnosis has been a contributory factor to the disproportionately lengthy stay Deaf people spend as in-patients. Denmark's study found that he, as the consultant psychiatrist at the Whittingham Hospital Deaf Unit, agreed with the diagnostic label in only five out of twenty-eight cases referred to him by other psychiatrists.

In general, the diagnostic procedures at Springfield and Whittingham differ. At Springfield, patients tend to be seen by a number of professionals, whereas at Whittingham, the initial diagnosis is made by the consultant psychiatrist. Another major difference between the hospitals is the position each adopts regarding the use of psychotherapy as a valid form of treatment. Whittingham, like the National Association for Mental Health (MIND), is very sceptical of the 'Talking Cure', whereas Springfield sees this as a major area for development with patients. Busfield and Ellenberger are very critical of psychotherapy as a treatment option. Rack sees it as a valid option only for a limited number of cultural groups, excluding by implication marginalized groups such as Black people and Deaf people.

ITQ

We have presented a picture of Deaf people being processed by a mental health system alien to them and operated by hearing professionals. But why should this be problematic for Deaf people? When we talk of differences in language, culture and communication needs, exactly what are these differences and how do they lead to disadvantage for Deaf people? List some of the factors that operate in a deaf–hearing interaction within the mental health system, and think about how they might manufacture a disadvantage for Deaf people.

◄ Comment

Your list may contain such factors as:

mis-communication

cultural misunderstanding

a stereotyped view of the abilities of Deaf people

a medical model view of deafness as dysfunction

Bear these in mind as you read through the next section, and consider to what extent these difficulties might be resolved by the introduction into the mental health system of Deaf people as professionals. ◄

12 Deaf professionals within the mental health system

If the therapist is able to communicate fluently in sign language, possess a working knowledge of the psychological aspects of deafness, understand the social reality of the deaf individual, and holds a positive attitude toward deafness and sign language, he or she can hope to be an effective therapist with deaf people.

(Brauer and Sussman, 1980, in Elliott *et al.*, 1987)

Harris (in Elliott *et al.*, 1987) believes that Deaf therapists have a unique contribution to make in helping Deaf people with emotional issues: 'their fluency in manual communication and their intimate knowledge of the deaf culture … make them … invaluable'. However, there are currently no Deaf psychiatrists in Britain, no psychiatrists with any degree of fluency in BSL, and no Deaf doctors in our mental health system. There are, though, a number of other Deaf professionals working in the two Deaf units and elsewhere. What role do they play professionally, and do they, as Harris suggests, provide something unique?

◄ Video
Now watch Video Three again. This time pay attention to Herbert Marvin, the deaf counsellor from Springfield Hospital. Does he feel Deaf professionals have a role to play within our mental health system? ◄

Herbert Marvin very much emphasizes the importance of Deaf professionals, especially of therapists and counsellors. Yet how many are there in the UK? Both Springfield and Whittingham Hospitals employ Deaf occupational therapists. Springfield has two Deaf counsellors, whilst Whittingham employs two Deaf people as instructors/facilitators, in much the same way as does the Hayfields Rehabilitation Unit in Glasgow. The total number of full-time posts filled by Deaf professionals within the mental health system is around seventeen. This figure includes the smaller longer stay establishments such as Richardson House and Court Grange. There is no doubt that many Deaf people employed in non-therapeutic roles do perform important, albeit informal, therapeutic functions. In Section 1 we discussed the various psychiatric facilities available to Deaf people such as Hayfields and Richardson House. It might be useful at this stage to re-read that section.

In Video Three Herbert Marvin suggests that much distress could be prevented if Deaf people were able to gain access to non-statutory services much earlier on, rather than being delayed and then having to go to a psychiatric hospital. In other words, they should have the same ease of access to services such as doctors, social workers, welfare or pastoral workers, psychologists, counsellors and nursing staff, as do hearing people. Marvin also emphasizes that too many Deaf people, who could be seen in non-medical settings if these existed, end up in psychiatric care.

Sachs *et al.* (1972) believe that a Deaf–Deaf interaction during the therapeutic process allows for clear 'identification'; in other words, both the Deaf client and the Deaf therapist have a shared feeling of, 'you know what I mean, you've been there yourself'. Langholtz (in Elliott *et al.*, 1987) suggests that 'identification' means a shared language. However, there are regional variations in BSL, and Deaf people can also choose to communicate by other methods (as Units 2 and 3 have shown). So how can one reconcile the views of Langholtz and Sachs without there being a clear uniformity of language, culture and experience?

Elliott *et al.* (1987) also point to a number of difficulties facing Deaf professionals working in the mental health field: a Deaf therapist may be viewed by the client or the family as less competent; the client cannot so easily claim to be misunderstood by another Deaf person, so may feel threatened; sign systems and communication methods may not be congruent and may lead to early disappointment; and there is the risk both of over-identification with the client, and of the 'rush' to establish a deep and meaningful relationship with the therapist because he or she is also Deaf.

Rampton is a high security psychiatric hospital resembling more a prison than a conventional hospital. Janet Goodwill is a Deaf person employed at Rampton as a sign language teacher. Her role within the institution is graphically described in Reader One. Her account (with Rae Than) describes the input a Deaf professional has made to the Deaf patients and the effect this has had on her hearing colleagues.

◀ Reading
Janet Goodwill and Rae Than's account 'Provision for Deaf Patients in Rampton Special Hospital', can be found in Reader One, Article 25. Read this carefully. Make notes on how Rampton staff and Goodwill have accommodated each other. Do any of the pitfalls mentioned earlier by Elliott *et al.* arise in Goodwill and Than's account? ◀

Goodwill and Than's account seems to suggest that the appointment of a Deaf person has influenced both staff and patients—'... The impact of Janet's arrival was instant and dramatic'— and Goodwill received 'an astonishing sixty applications' from staff to start sign language classes. The introduction of a Deaf professional into the system may produce unforeseen difficulties, especially considering the comparatively passive position occupied by deaf people in relation to hearing people, particularly within the medical establishment. Goodwill and Than note that some of the problem areas arise from 'unspoken rules' and 'professional jargon'. In other words, Goodwill did not have access to the language of her professional colleagues and difficulties arose when she felt she needed an interpreter for staff meetings. There are parallels here with deaf teachers of the deaf, as outlined in Unit 5 and Janice Silo's Article 19 in Reader One, which you read in conjunction with Unit 5.

Elliott *et al.* (1987) emphasize the need for access to an interpreter for Deaf people, especially for supervision, which is an essential ingredient to the development of professional competence. Elliott *et al.* and Goodwill and Than emphasize the importance of good and direct communication between Deaf and hearing colleagues, though they accept that this is sometimes difficult. Schlesinger and Meadows (in Elliott *et al.*, 1987) describe the scenario in which hearing people avoid what they perceive as stressful interaction with Deaf colleagues, as 'shock-withdrawal paralysis'; in other words, anxiety in the hearing person causes communication to break down completely. Elliott *et al.* suggest that the Deaf person ought to 'rescue' the situation: 'In such circumstances, the Deaf professional must facilitate the communication process by offering reassurance and communication options' (Elliott *et al.*, 1987). This does, however, place the onus of responsibility upon the Deaf person rather than on a negotiated process between two individuals.

In Block 1, the diversity of the Deaf population was clearly demonstrated, yet hearing people will tend to assume that a Deaf person is an expert or authority about deafness and all aspects of Deaf culture. This may or may not be true. Elliott *et al.* (1987) refer to this behaviour by hearing people as the 'instant expert' process.

There is little or no evidence of the actual, or indeed potential, role that Deaf professionals could play with hearing patients. Their generally good communication skills may help them to be effective with a wide range of patients both hearing and Deaf. Herbert Marvin (Video Three) felt that Deaf people do not have access to the necessary non-statutory therapeutic services within the community, and therefore find themselves in psychiatric care. Could services for Deaf people be made more available and within the community? In the next section we will look at the care-in-the-community debate and discuss its relevance to Deaf people.

13 Community care

We cannot perfect the asylum because its very existence embodies a contradiction—the central contradiction of psychiatry itself, that between care and custody. Psychiatry, both as theory and practise, has overtly the medical goal of promoting health but is compromised by its role in controlling deviance and maintaining public order.

(Basaglia, in Ingleby, 1981)

This powerful and remarkable statement characterized the mood of the anti-psychiatry movement of the 1970s. Psychiatric services until quite recently have been concentrated in large NHS hospitals; they seem set to change but we do not as yet know how the various proposals will be implemented and how these may affect Deaf consumers.

Is the anti-psychiatry movement, as epitomized by Basaglia, idealist and utopian, or can we indeed develop alternatives to hospital care based within the community? Community care will mean different things to different people. For example, it might mean something approximating a social Darwinist model; that is, where the fittest patients survive and thrive, whilst others, presumably, fail. Or perhaps it might mean the establishment of thousands of neighbourhood-based statutory services. These two models are extremes and are presented here to emphasize the vast diversity of possible forms of community care. We begin this section by looking at some theories on the development of community care and then at how current proposals might manifest themselves during the 1990s.

In *Managing Madness*, Busfield (1986) maps out the move away from the institutional care of psychiatric patients to community-based alternatives. Busfield presents two competing explanations for the post-war move to community care. First, there is the 'standard' account, which identifies the development of synthetic drugs in the 1950s as the main reason: this enabled some patients to be treated in the community rather than in hospital. Second, there was a recognition that institutional care was less therapeutic than the patient's own home environment.

In contrast to this is Scull's analysis of this shift (Scull, 1977), the basis of his argument being the economic rationale. He identifies two major weaknesses with the 'standard' account: (i) the number of residents in psychiatric hospitals was already in decline by the time the 'new' drugs started to appear in the mid 1950s; and (ii) there is little evidence to suggest that 'anti-psychotic' medicines have any real curative effect on mental illness. Instead, Scull maintains that the real reason for the move to community care, or 'decarceration' as he terms it, is that institutional, segregative forms of social control became too expensive. Patients were simply put back into the community to survive as best they could, rather than to be helped to rehabilitate as the rhetoric of community care claims.

Whilst sharing Scull's concern that community care has been mystified in an attempt to cover a general tenor of neglect, Busfield rejects Scull's analysis on two points. In his opinion: (i) Scull fails to take into account the pattern of development of mental health services this century, particularly the development of services outside of psychiatric hospitals; and (ii) the fiscal crisis which underpins Scull's analysis was a feature of the 1970s and not of the 1950s, when anxiety regarding institutional cost was not a determinant of expenditure.

Busfield's own analysis of the shift to community care rests on a notion of a 'new model' of care for psychiatric patients which began to take shape before the Second World War:

> First, the emergence of new medical ideas of the causes and treatment of mental illness undermined the support for and commitment to institutions as the desirable locus of care explicit in earlier environmentalist thinking about insanity. Second, the development of a broader range of state funded services and benefits, not only eliminated the institutional bias of the welfare system, but also increasingly made institutional care seem neither necessary nor appropriate. Third, the new model of care offered opportunities to psychiatrists for a fuller integration of their specialism with the rest of medicine and a close approximation of their practise to that of the parent discipline. Fourth, the therapeutic optimism generated by the therapeutic innovations of the 1930s, 1940s and 1950s made shorter stays in hospital and adequate out-patients care seem a practical proposition.
>
> (Busfield, 1986)

There is an interesting parallel here with the proposals to change the custodial care of offenders. Throughout the 1980s the already over-crowded prison population has steadily risen. The government has sought an alternative to the 'soft option' of probation; one of these is the use of heavier fines and electronic tagging. For those who are considered 'unsafe' a new option may well be 'private prisons' based on an American model. These are cheaper to run and are without a therapeutic component. These new prisons in turn have interesting parallels with many private psychiatric hospitals in Britain prior to the establishment of the NHS!

It is fashionable to talk about community care and the abolition of psychiatric hospitals, but in practice how will the new structure develop? Who will fund it, what will happen to institutional resources and what do we mean by 'community care'?

Italy is the only country to have taken steps in law to abolish the 'asylum'. The pressure for this radical action was prompted by the strong anti-psychiatric movement of the late 1970s headed by Franco Basaglia of Trieste, Northern Italy. The experiment of 'freeing' patients into the community failed and within 2 years the Act of Parliament was repealed. What went wrong and are there valuable lessons we could learn in this country?

Central to Basaglia's thinking was that 'patients had to be given back their rights as citizens' and 'one measure of citizenship is the power of franchise' (Basaglia, in Ingleby, 1981). It was not until the 1982 Mental Health Amendment Act that psychiatric patients were given the right to vote in this country. Basaglia explains that it is not the bricks and mortar of the hospital that create the institution but the relationship the patient has to the rest of society. Without rights, without income and without an autonomous identity, the patient within a 'total institution' such as a psychiatric hospital is no longer a full citizen of the state.

The Trieste experiment has lessons that many of us can learn. First, patients must be allowed to be complete citizens. Second, without support within the community, ex-patients will fail to thrive. And third, society must allow both the old and the new structures to run in parallel for a period of transition to allow for professionals, patients and wider society to assimilate the changes.

In reference to the 1983 Mental Health Act, John Hamilton makes the following point: 'Under this new act patients have better rights than before, but with no new resources and the current constraints on the National Health Service, these rights may prove to be meaningless and patients may be worse off in terms of getting the treatment they need' (Hamilton, 1983).

The same sentiments are also currently being echoed by observers regarding the government's community care programme. Local authorities had their incomes severely reduced and regulated by central government throughout the 1980s by rate-capping, reductions in the rate-support grant and the implementation of the community charge. Coupled with implementation of expensive legislation such as The Disabled Persons Act 1986 and The Children Act 1989, local authorities may not be able to continue to provide current services, such as education, social services and housing, at the same level.

The 1980s saw the mapping out of a Thatcherite version of community care. As far as the health service is concerned, this process started in 1982, when area health authorities were dispensed with after an 8-year existence. The following year, the Department of Health and Social Security's 'NHS Management Enquiry' was set up and the report of this enquiry (known as the Griffiths Report, after the name of its chair and author) was published in 1988 as *Community Care: Agenda For Action*.

The 1986 Audit Commission Report *Making a Reality of Community Care* had expressed concern over the way that local authorities were funding their community care programmes. This, coupled with the government's obsession with 'value for money in the public sector' argument, provided the context within which Griffiths would approach his task. Not surprisingly, Griffiths strongly recommended that the public sector should implement rational business methods learned from the private sector (Sir Roy Griffith's background is as managing director of Sainsbury's), in cutting waste and improving efficiency.

The report is, in fact, only Griffiths' view of what community care in the future could be, as no research was undertaken or consultation programmes implemented. When it was completed there was an attempt by the government to 'hide it', as one of the recommendations was that funds be transferred from central government to local government in order to finance community care programmes, and it was wrongly interpreted by the press as being an anti-Thatcher document. In reality, Sir Roy had simply taken so long to produce his slim (only 36 pages) report, that in the meantime the world had changed, the Department of Health and Social Security had become the Department of Health, and the power of local authorities was being reduced by central government almost on a daily basis.

It is the government's expressed intention that local authorities diversify their role to include becoming managers and inspectors of services that are provided by voluntary, independent or private organizations. According to Roger Freeman MP, Parliamentary Secretary for Health, 1989, the government's policy on mental illness:

> ... is to encourage co-operation between the NHS and private sector, particularly when it involves a cost-effective way of providing or extending services.

> ... The government's long-standing policy is that people with a mental illness should have access to all the services they need as locally as possible.

> ... One of our key tasks in the field of community care is to encourage the development of a fully integrated range of services, specifically tailored to the needs of the elderly, the mentally ill and the mentally handicapped. Our community care policy is therefore aimed at ensuring that people who need care and support receive it in appropriate settings.

> (Freeman, 1989)

Freeman's speech contains many diverse stands: privatization, local services and integrated provision. But, bearing in mind the geographical spread of Deaf people, it raises serious questions of feasibility with regard to community care.

Basaglia's analysis of the failure of the Trieste experiment gave a clear warning that the structures need sufficient time to adapt and adequate funds to respond. However, little money appears to be directed towards developing community-based resources, according to Dr Birley, President of the Royal College of Psychiatrists. He estimates that 80 to 90 per cent of mental health money is still tied up in hospitals and the amount of money for mental health has not increased in 'real terms' since 1974 (*The Guardian*, 14 March 1990).

The government's decision not to implement Section 7 of the Disabled Persons Act 1986 is seen as a set-back for many psychiatric patients returning to the community. Essentially, Section 7 places a duty on health authorities to inform social services to plan a menu of community provision. Without prior notice, many patients may find themselves homeless, jobless and without money when discharged from hospital.

MIND (The National Association for Mental Health), the largest voluntary organization representing mentally ill people, has developed a model for psychiatric community care. MIND describes community care for patients as requiring a 'holistic service' which would include the following elements. It would be:

- △ local and accessible
- △ individualized and consumerist
- △ co-ordinated and accountable
- △ friendly and non-stigmatizing
- △ appropriate and flexible
- △ not segregated and available

In *Building Better Futures*, MIND (1989) did not reach the same conclusion as Basaglia on the continuing, albeit changed role of the psychiatric hospital: 'Hospitals and acute units would not be needed in the future because people in crisis would be able to go to refuges and places of asylum in the community' (MIND, 1989). What is not clear is what these new crisis centres would be like and how they would be funded. Basaglia *et al.* recommended that existing psychiatric hospitals be used as places of asylum and safety when care within the community was not available or appropriate.

At the time of writing, the two White Papers, 'Agenda for Action' and 'Working for Patients', are now before Parliament as a single Bill, 'The NHS and Community Care Bill, 1989'.

Figure 6.4 Individual therapy at Richardson House
(Source: courtesy of the Royal National Institute for the Deaf)

What are the implications of the Bill for Deaf people? Potentially these would be the same as for hearing people, in that there might be a movement from local authority and NHS provision to community-based, non-statutory services such as the voluntary or private sectors. There are some significant characteristics of current services for Deaf people that may affect the style of potential changes. There are only two psychiatric hospitals for Deaf people, two long-stay rehabilitation centres and a tiny handful of out-patient services. Services for Deaf people are also different in that much of the long-stay provision and community social work is already provided by the voluntary sector. Much of the ideology contained within the Griffiths Report and the NHS and Community Care Bill is already present within current services for Deaf people.

We have already said that Deaf people generally spend longer periods of time as in-patients than do hearing people and that very few of these in-patients are diagnosed as having serious psychiatric illness. One possible outcome may well be the proliferation of semi-independent living schemes supported by unit staff. Financial restrictions may well also mean that the length of stay as an in-patient will be significantly reduced. An important development has been the establishment of a cluster of semi-independent facilities around Springfield Hospital. Yet this still has at its centre a psychiatric hospital. Therefore, can these facilities be regarded as truly community based?

The future of the two Deaf units is not completely secure. The Whittingham Unit, near Preston, is under pressure to move to Manchester and to provide more community-based services. Springfield has received supra-regional funding to establish additional facilities for a child and adolescent unit. There are also longer-term aims to establish a child guidance unit for deaf children and their families in London.

A substantial proportion of social work is provided to the Deaf community by locally based charitable agencies under contract from the local authority (approximately 25 per cent). The principle of contracted services certainly looks to be extended in the near future, therefore much of the existing service is unlikely to change. It is not clear how local authority provision will be affected. For example, it is conceivable that a large charitable organization, such as the RNID, could step in and contract much of current local authority services for Deaf people. How this might affect the quality of services is unclear.

ITQ

If one or more large charities such as the RNID or the National Deaf Children's Society (NDCS) undertook to become a major provider of services at a national level, how would this new role be accommodated with their traditional one of being advocate and watchdog? Can campaigning and consumer groups become service providers without a certain amount of role conflict? How might this scenario affect a national charity representing Deaf people and its relationship to Deaf people?

You might like to think about these questions now, and bear them in mind. This issue will be dealt with in more detail in Unit 7.

---

14 Conclusions

◀ Activity 3

In the Introduction we stated that we would not be investigating Deaf people within the mental health system, instead we would be looking at the underpinning of current practice and policy. You were asked to bear in mind two key questions throughout work on this unit:

(a) What are the major factors that influence the way in which Deaf people are perceived by psychiatric personnel?

and

(b) Should the personal and social problems of Deaf people be the concern of psychiatric personnel?

Go back to your original notes on these two questions and review your answers in the light of the work you have done on the unit so far. Make some further notes before proceeding. ◀

There are only two psychiatric hospitals in the UK working specifically with Deaf people, one near Preston, the other in London. There are also a few long-stay residential centres with a strong rehabilitation tradition; the Hayfields Unit in Glasgow is an example of one these.

Despite the fact that, as Denmark points out, 'deaf people are no more likely to suffer from frank mental illness than the hearing population', their average length of stay in general psychiatric hospitals, as in-patients, is around 20 years, compared to several months for a hearing person.

The way in which Deaf people are referred to specialist psychiatric centres could be said to be unique. Denmark found that the majority of referrals made to the Whittingham Hospital were from Social Workers with Deaf People, whereas a hearing person almost certainly would be referred to a consultant psychiatrist by their general practitioner.

Once at the specialist Deaf units, the majority of Deaf people are diagnosed as having severe behavioural problems or disorders. The treatment generally prescribed for these patients is rehabilitation, which mostly consists of education and life skills training. The question we have posed throughout this unit is, 'Why are people, who mostly require rehabilitation, resident as in-patients in a psychiatric hospital?'. We have suggested that this may be because:

1   There are only two Deaf units in the UK. Where else would a Deaf person with a behavioural disorder requiring rehabilitation be referred?

2   The costs of establishing a range of local rehabilitation centres would be very expensive for a handful of Deaf people. Referral to supra-regional centres is, therefore, more attractive financially.

The initial diagnostic procedure between the two specialist psychiatric units differs. Springfield tends to use a multi-disciplinary approach, whereas Whittingham adopts a more conventional approach based on the opinion of the consultant psychiatrist. Another difference between the two hospitals is their use of psychotherapy as a treatment option. Whittingham, like MIND, rejects the 'Talking Cure', whereas Springfield is investing increasingly more of its resources in developing psychotherapy with Deaf patients.

The medical model view of deafness, as a dysfunction or sickness, has influenced the way in which doctors have tended to view deafness, rather than focusing on the Deaf person's needs. One outcome of the medical model of analysis was the development of the concept of surdophrenia, or Deaf mind. Whilst this concept attracted much attention post-war, there is no empirical evidence to support it. Having said that, it continues to be endorsed by a number of professionals.

Is there such a thing as a 'psychology of the Deaf'? Rodda and Denmark believe so. In the well-known study, *A Word in Deaf Ears,* they set out to develop the concept and offer it as a working paradigm of analysis and treatment. Harlan Lane, amongst others, is very critical of attempts to develop a psychology of the Deaf. He points out that the validity of the study is questionable, first on empirical grounds, and second, because the testing procedure could not have elicited the desired response from Deaf people on both cultural and linguistic grounds.

According to Rose, one of the tasks for early psychologists was to find some way of marking differences between individuals, and to identify those whose behaviour appeared to stray from the 'expected or conventional'. Foucault identifies the shift from corporal punishment of offenders or deviants towards a model based on individualized disciplining of the transgressor's mind as a crucial step in the later development of prisons, hospitals and schools. The development of the mental sciences in the twentieth century has been characterized by notions of individualization and normalization, and these ideas have become embedded within the practice of the mental health system.

The origins of the British mental health system can be traced back to the early parts of nineteenth century but the events heralding its birth are determined by why, rather than how, it developed. The changing style of provision from private care to statutory hospital-based services, and then more recently towards a model of care in the community, has attracted different explanations. Scull locates the rationale as being linked with the changing pattern of the national economy. When the economy is depressed, cheaper community-based resources are developed instead. Busfield explains the changing patterns in terms of (a) the introduction of new drugs, allowing patients to be cared for in the community; and (b) changes in professional practice which appear to suggest that care outside of institutions might be more therapeutic.

The anti-psychiatry movement felt that hospitals took away patients' rights as citizens; alternatives to incarceration needed to be sought. Basaglia suggests that the contradictory nature of psychiatry itself—that is, between care and control—prevents it from achieving its intended goal of care.

Care within the community is popular with all political sides but no agreed definition of community care has yet been achieved. Service provision will depend largely on the prevailing ideology of the decision makers. One cannot predict the scale or style of future services. We can only say that they appear certain to change, creating new roles for local authorities and

NHS managers, from service providers to roles that would include acting as planning, funding and inspecting agents for services provided by private, independent and voluntary organizations.

There are no Deaf psychiatrists or Deaf doctors working in our mental health system and the role played by Deaf people has only recently begun to be developed. At present most Deaf people are employed as facilitators, educators or communicators, who play informal, albeit significant, therapeutic roles such as counsellors. Video Three shows the Deaf staff at Springfield working with a group of Deaf patients.

Are Deaf people in a position to play a significant role in services delivered to other Deaf people both at a preventative and at a remedial level, whether in specialist centres or within the community?

Herbert Marvin on Video Three comments:

> I feel strongly that more Deaf people should work in psychiatry to help people better. There would be less mental illness because Deaf people would be able to sort out the problems of Deaf patients. I also feel that more Deaf staff would actually help hearing professionals to learn more about deafness because hearing people do not have enough exposure, do not learn enough about Deaf people, so it would be good for Deaf and hearing people to work together. I think it would be better, there would be more information, many, many things would improve.

References

BASILIER, T. (1964a) in *Acta Psychiatrica Scandinavica Supplementum*, 40, pp. 362–74.

BASILIER, T. (1964b) 'Surdophrenia', in Gregory, S. and Hartley, G.M. (eds) (1990) *Constructing Deafness*, London, Pinter Publishers. (D251 Reader Two, Article 3.3)

BRITISH DEAF ASSOCIATION (1984) *1983 Mental Health Act and Deaf Patients*, Carlisle, British Deaf Association.

BUSFIELD, J. (1986) *Managing Madness*, London, Unwin Hyman.

CLARE, A. (1980) *Psychiatry in Dissent*, London, Tavistock.

DENMARK, J. (1966) 'Mental illness and early profound deafness', in *British Journal of Medical Psychology*, no. 39, p. 117.

DENMARK, J. (1972) 'Surdophrenia', in *Sound,* vol. 6, no. 4, November.

DENMARK, J. (1985) 'A study of 250 patients referred to a department of psychiatry for the deaf', in *The British Journal of Psychiatry*, vol. 146, March.

DENMARK, J., RODDA, M., ABEL, A., SKELTON, V., ELDRIDGE, W., WARREN, F. and GORDON, A. (1979) *A Word in Deaf Ears*, London, RNID.

DENMARK, J. and WARREN, F. (1972) 'A psychiatric unit for the deaf', in *The British Journal of Psychiatry*, vol. 120, no. 557, April.

ELLIOTT, H., GLASS, L. and EVANS, J.W. (1987) *Mental Health Assessments of Deaf Clients*, Boston, MA, Little, Brown and Company.

FOUCAULT, M. (1979) *Discipline and Punish*, London, Peregrine.

FREEMAN, R. (1989) Charter Nightingale Lecture, 5 September, on the future of psychiatric services.

GOODWILL, J. and THAN, R. (1990) 'Provision for deaf patients in Rampton Special Hospital', in Taylor, G. and Bishop, J. (eds) (1990) *Being Deaf: The Experience of Deafness*, London, Pinter Publishers. (D251 Reader One, Article 25)

GREGORY, S. and HARTLEY, G. (eds) (1990) *Constructing Deafness*, London, Pinter Publishers. (D251 Reader Two)

HAMILTON, J. (1983) in *British Medical Journal*, vol. 286, 28 May.

HIGGINS, P. (1980) *Outsiders in a Hearing World*, Beverly Hills, CA, Sage.

ILLICH, I. (1975) *Medical Nemesis*, London, Caldar and Boyars.

INGLEBY, D. (1981) *Critical Psychiatry: The Politics of Mental Health*, London, Penguin.

KYLE, J. (1983) 'Looking for meaning in sign language sentences', in Gregory, S. and Hartley, G.M. (eds) (1990) *Constructing Deafness*, London, Pinter Publishers. (D251 Reader Two, Article 3.2)

LANE, H. (1988) 'Is there a "psychology of the deaf"?', in Gregory, S. and Hartley, G.M. (eds) (1990) *Constructing Deafness*, London, Pinter Publishers. (D251 Reader Two, Article 3.4)

LEVINE, E. (1956) *Youth in a Soundless World*, New York, Columbia University Press.

MILLER, P. AND ROSE, N. (eds) (1986) *The Power of Psychiatry*, Cambridge, Polity Press.

MIND (NATIONAL ASSOCIATION FOR MENTAL HEALTH) (1974) *Psychotherapy: Do We Need More 'Talking Treatment'?* Report no. 12, London, MIND.

MIND (NATIONAL ASSOCIATION FOR MENTAL HEALTH) (1989) *Building Better Futures,* London, MIND.

MORAITIS, S. (1979) 'Migrants', in Bates, E.M. and Wilson, P.R. (eds) *Mental Disorder or Madness*, St Lucia, Queensland, University of Queensland Press.

MYKLEBUST, H. (1960) *The Psychology of Deafness*, New York, Grune and Stratton.

PARKER, I. (1989) 'Discourse and power', in Shotter, J. and Gergen, K.J. (eds) *Texts of Identity*, London, Sage.

POTTER, J. AND WETHERELL, M. (1987) *Discourse and Social Psychology*, London, Sage.

QUIGLEY, S. and PAUL, P. (1984) 'Cognition and language', in Gregory, S. and Hartley, G.M. (eds) (1990) *Constructing Deafness*, London, Pinter Publishers. (D251 Reader Two, Article 3.1)

RACK, P. (1982) *Race, Culture and Mental Disorder*, London, Tavistock Publications.

RAINER, J. and ALTSHULER, K. (1967) *Psychiatry and the Deaf*, Washington, DC, US Department of Health, Education and Welfare.

RODDA, M. and GROVE, C. (1987) *Language, Cognition and Deafness*, Hillsdale, NJ, Laurence Erlbaum Associates.

ROSE, N. (1989) 'Individualizing psychology', in Shotter, J. and Gergen, K.J. (eds) *Texts of Identity*, London, Sage.

SACHS, B., DITTMAN, A. and SUSSMAN, A. (1972) 'Psychological interviewing with deaf clients', *Journal of the Rehabilitation of the Deaf*, vol. 6, pp. 140–55.

SCULL, A. (1977) *Decarceration*, Englewood Cliffs, NJ, Prentice-Hall.

SEDGWICK, P. (1982) *Psychopolitics*, London, Pluto Press.

TAYLOR, G. and BISHOP, J. (eds) (1990) *Being Deaf: The Experience of Deafness*, London, Pinter Publishers. (D251 Reader One)

TIMMERMANS, L. (1988) Report to the Congress Meeting of the European Society for Mental Health and Deafness.

Acknowledgements

Grateful acknowledgement is made to the following sources for permission to reproduce material in this unit:

Figures

Figures 6.1, 6.2, 6.3, 6.4 The Royal National Institute for the Deaf.

Grateful acknowledgement is made to Trevor Landell for permission to use his painting on the covers and title pages throughout the units of this course.